How to Be a Movie Star,

or
A Terrible Beauty Is Born

Chris Chase

How
to Be a
Movie Star,
or
A Terrible
Beauty Is
Born

Harper & Row, Publishers
New York Evanston
San Francisco
London

Grateful acknowledgment is made for permission to reprint excerpts from the following material:

"Leda and the Swan" by William Butler Yeats as published in *Collected Poems*. Copyright 1928 by Macmillan Publishing Co., Inc., renewed 1956 by George Yeats. Reprinted by permission of Macmillan Publishing Co., Inc., M. B. Yeats, Miss Anne Yeats and MacMillan Co. of Canada.

"A Song" by William Butler Yeats as published in *Collected Poems*. Copyright 1919 by Macmillan Publishing Co., Inc., renewed 1947 by Bertha Georgie Yeats. Reprinted by permission of Macmillan Publishing Co., Inc., M. B. Yeats, Miss Anne Yeats and MacMillan Co. of Canada.

FIRST EDITION

Designed by Dorothy Schmiderer.

Library of Congress Cataloging in Publication Data

Chase, Chris.
    How to be a movie star.
    1. Chase, Chris. 2. Actresses—Correspondence, reminiscences, etc. I. Title.
PN2287.C52A33   791'.092'4 [B]   72–9750
ISBN 0–06–010726–X

Contents

For Mike Chase

Foreword

Perhaps the reader noticed a little collaboration between me and William Butler Yeats when it come to the title of this book. I would have liked to use a quotation from him in the front of every chapter, and put his name on the cover, too, but I couldn't take the chance. Poetry don't sell.

It's nothing against the man—*poeta nascitur, non fit:* W.B. couldn't help it—but I am hoping to make a lot of money as a writer because I have been an actor since 1955 and there is only seventeen dollars in my pension fund.

The writing game is less convivial than the acting game— no applause, no roses, no roistering through the gorgeous words of a genius: you're stuck within the limits of your own vision—yet I came to believe this book had to be written. Because I took an advance and spent it on caps for my front teeth.

The enterprise began a couple of years ago, when a wise and beautiful newspaper editor named Sy Peck printed (in the Sunday drama section of *The New York Times*) a wise and beautiful article I had written about my life in art. It caught my agent's attention. (Up till then, my agent had been treating me like Marlene Dietrich treated guys in *Shanghai Express*, showing them the door while murmuring, "I'm wee wee of you now.")

So my agent started talking about books. She said anybody could write a book and look all the dopes that do. "They," she said, referring to New York publishers, "are always looking for a tale told by an idiot or a midget or a ballplayer."

And I'm no midget or no ballplayer, so I can't think what she meant.

The only thing I'm a hundred percent sure of is that the caps on my front teeth aren't holding up too good. Still, I choose to defy augury.

1

My Father and Other Old Blocks

I come from a theatrical tradition.

Every New Year's Eve, my father got dressed in a diaper, with a rose in his teeth. And my brother Paul used to hang around the kitchen acting out the plots of movies, starting with a title and a fanfare. *"Frankenstein vee-essis the Wolf-Man—* Heart-rendering! soul-rendering! epic!"

The reason Paul wouldn't come out of the kitchen was that a bigger kid named Egan had threatened to stretch him.

"Can he do it?" Paul would ask. "Can he stretch me?"

To be honest, we didn't know. We didn't know whether Egan was being poetic, or whether he had a rack. We didn't know what my brother had done to provoke Egan. All we knew was that Paul refused to go to school anymore. No arguments, threats or kicks in the behind would change his mind.

The kids in the neighborhood loved playacting, even the sissy boy up the block who was kept so clean you could eat off him, and the tough little girl named Winifred, who leaned toward games of lust.

In first grade, I got up and told the class my father was an actress, and when they laughed I was offended. I didn't see anything funny about it.

Across the street from the house where we lived during my earliest years, there were two children's museums, in two little parks. One museum was a sort of natural-history building in which children sat for hours, bent over jigsaw puzzles.

The way it worked was you were sent down into the cellar to wash your hands—I once washed my mother's topaz ring right down the drain—and then you came back up and showed your hands, tops and bottoms, to a person in charge. If you passed the clean test, you were given a lovely-smelling cedar box which contained big fat pieces of a wooden jigsaw puzzle. You would go sit at a table, put your puzzle together and, when it was done, you would discover you had fashioned, say, a hairy grosbeak. You would then get up and walk around the room until you found a stuffed replica of your bird behind one of the sealed-in showcases covering the walls. And you would study the information on the fact sheet that stood beside the replica.

As soon as you had memorized the news that the hairy grosbeak weighed fourteen pounds, never sang in captivity, ate only muenster cheese and was a faithful mate, you would go back to the person who'd okayed your clean hands and say to him or her, "Hairy grosbeak." He or she would walk over to the table, check that your puzzle was really finished, then ask you hairy grosbeak questions. If you answered them correctly, you got a point. These points were entered on cards in an index-card file, and at some future date, when you'd amassed maybe a thousand of them, you won a prize. I think the prize was a hairy grosbeak in a cedar box.

It was pretty educational.

The other museum, the non-natural-history one, had a library with a bay window where you could curl up in a window seat and pretend you were eating an apple (I'd read that the pinnacle of happiness was to curl up in a window seat with a book and an apple).

Downstairs from the library, there was a little movie theatre. For some reason, I always expected them to be showing Joan

Crawford in a long dress sipping sherry wine, and they caught me again and again with shorts about How Bees Make Honey. I kept going and hoping.

The parks around the museums were interesting too. Once a lady approached me and asked if I knew where babies came from, and then she and I walked through the trees together, while she told me about eggs and fertilization and scared me silly.

When I went home and gave my father the baby lecture, he said that the lady should be arrested.

It was nothing to what he said about the delivery boy.

I'd been running home one afternoon when the delivery boy stopped me and asked if I knew how to perform a certain act.

I didn't like to look dumb, so I said sure, we'd learned it in school.

His eyes bugged out a little, but he suggested we go around in back of the museum. I said I was sorry, I had to get home, and tore away without even waving good-bye.

When I told my father *this* story, he phoned the police, and they sent over a detective who asked me questions about my delivery boy friend. How tall was he? How heavy was he? Did he have any distinguishing features?

Height and weight weren't concepts to me, so I panicked. I didn't know if my father was three feet two, or seven feet even.

"He was about your size," I said to the detective.

Asked point-blank what he'd looked like, the face of my would-be buddy went right out of my mind. So I invented him. He wound up with a bushy head of hair and a thin scar running from his Adam's apple to his earlobe. He weighed about 250 pounds, give or take a hundred, and, for all I know, they're searching for him yet.

I was a long, stringy kid with fine, mousy hair cut very short

3

because my mother believed constant shearing would cause it to grow in thick and abundant, and once a child in the street, viewing my passage, cried out, "Hey, Ma, is it a boy or a girl?" which cut me to the heart.

Secretly I yearned to be named Cynthia, and to have long golden curls, so that men would be mad about me. Whatever that meant.

I knew it had something to do with burning lips.

I was not only short-haired, I was hollow-eyed from sneaking out of bed nights to read forbidden books, and I worshiped a girl named Sylvia who wore a fresh cotton dress to school every day and whose long pigtails shone from brushing. She and her cousin Billy could play duets at the piano, and when they got home from school in the afternoon, they were given Mallomars and milk, and money for the Good Humor man.

I hung around these people for a while, taking handouts, but doing it with a certain amount of *délicatesse*. I'd always refuse ice cream money from Sylvia's mother; I'd only take enough for orange ice.

(In my house the food tasted terrible, since they had a theory that whatever you hated was good for you. If melted cheese stuck to the roof of your mouth for forty-five minutes, melted cheese was what you got for lunch. I used to throw up every morning, right before I got dressed.)

Spindly-legged, secretive, scared to answer anybody who said hello, yet full of grandiose ideas, I went around wishing I was anyone but me. I wanted to be Sylvia, with the ordered life, or Claire, whose parents had forked out for singing lessons so she could murder "Ciribiribin," or a red-haired girl named Audrey, whose second-best friend I became. (Her first-best friend was jealous and put a caterpillar down my back.)

Audrey was the most admirable of children. She went to

4

church every twenty minutes, and she studied Latin on her own (even though we were only in the third grade) while her brother and I practiced spitting from a second-story window. Years later, I met Audrey on Wall Street. She hadn't changed much. She was on her lunch hour from a secretarial job, and she took me with her, and we wound up at a soup kitchen run by Presbyterians. We were given a sandwich, gulped it down, then raced upstairs to a chapel, where we spent the rest of her lunch hour singing "He Walks with Me and He Talks with Me and He Tells Me I Am His Own."

I never met her for lunch after that. I figured I wasn't good enough.

I was plenty good enough to be an actor, though. All *they* had to do was sit around and play cards all night, and throw jars of cold cream at their maids, and men would be mad about them. Such information as I had I'd gleaned from my father, who'd put in a stint as a vaudevillian. He swears he played the Palace, but one of his wives threw his scrapbooks away, so he can't prove it.

My father is a kind of egocentric pixie, with a gift for storytelling and games. Once, when my sister and I were small, he came into our room and announced that he was an ogre, and he was going to boil us and eat us, and we yelped and screeched and begged him to leave us alone and go cook the fairies at the bottom of his garden, or some such thing, and my father snorted. "You can't cook fairies," he said sternly. "They won't stay in the pot."

When I told him I longed to act, he always laughed. And when kids would come and ask if I could go to the movies, he would say, "No. If she wants to be an actress, she has to learn to suffer," and then he'd laugh some more.

Sometimes I think he's had the last laugh at that.

2

How to Become a High-Fashion Model

When anybody's attained such heights of prominence as I have —the butcher recognizes me instantly: "Why, hello, Mrs. Chase," he says, and the baker and the candlestick maker aren't far behind—people want to know how it's done. How did I get where I am today. Since I'm not a person who's piggy with her secrets, I think first I'll tell everybody how to become a high-fashion model.

It's the easiest thing out, as my grandma used to say.

You just sit around in a lobby on the upper East Side for a few minutes, and then this guy comes in with a camera.

Honest. I wouldn't lie about such a serious subject.

(Though I'm not sure interior gommints haven't had a lot to do with my success. I once met a lady who was head of a lingerie empire, and she fixed me with a steely eye and said, "The most fashionable clothes isn't gonna do for you if you haven't got the right interior gommint." I'm happy to say I never forgot these words of wisdom, and my interior gommints are always exquisite.)

But to get back to fashion modeling.

I'd finished high school, and had to go to work because my family pointed out that they'd been feeding me for better than fifteen years, which was a dog's age. (That's typical of my family.

6

They figured every one of a person's years was seven of a dog's, and if you multiply 15 by 7, you can see they'd made up their minds they'd been supporting me for 105 years.)

So I got a couple of jobs in rapid succession.

I went down to Wall Street and sat at a high stool and tried to keep up with a ticker-tape machine, transferring onto a great graph in front of me, by means of pencil and trembling fingers, any changes in the prices of any stocks. Every noon I would buy a frankfurter at Nedick's and go sit by the water down at the Battery and snivel into my hot dog, wondering how you got discovered for motion pictures when you were spending your entire life so far east of the studios, not to mention so far south of Fourteenth Street.

Then I changed jobs. I went to work at a publishing company. I was hired because I'd never heard of more than sixty dollars a week. The man who chose me had given a questionnaire and a test to a crowd of college girls, but they looked expensive and he was easily intimidated.

I was the answer to his prayers. Cowed, gum-chewing, knee-soxed, I stood giggling nervously throughout our interview, and he felt immensely relieved. Obviously I was not the kind of teen-ager to go on ski weekends, try to start a union or otherwise give a chap the vapors.

So our romance began.

I love that man. His name is Albert Delacorte, he's a first-rate writer who never writes, a crackerjack editor who no longer edits; he's presently teaching Puerto Ricans to speak English and denying, in his offhand Princeton manner, that he's really helping anybody.

Back in the days of his tenure at the Dell Publishing Company, he trained me to do various editorial jobs. I cut, edited, wrote. I wrote the lives of baseball stars, and advice on becoming a woman. I wrote about hairdos, and I wrote movie reviews. Once I got in trouble because a studio complained that I'd called Tony Curtis a greasy jerk. I hadn't. I'd described the character he was playing as a greasy jerk, and the character he was playing *was* a greasy jerk.

Albert always backed me up. He was crazy about oddballs. He even supported a few, including an old pal who'd had a lobotomy and who spent his subsequent days plotting the perfect murder of his mother.

While the lobotomy had relaxed all this fellow's inhibitions (he wouldn't have felt *guilty* about murdering his mother), fortunately it had also robbed him of the initiative the deed would have required.

What he was sore about was his mother had kept him from marrying the maid.

None of which has much to do with being a high-fashion model. I can see that myself. But I seem to have to tell a story from the very beginning, like my grandmother, who, if you asked her how she felt, informed you. People always knew more about my grandmother's arthritis than they had time for.

Anyway, one day Albert had sent me up to the fashionable East Side to interview Red Buttons, and I was sitting in the lobby of one of those great glass palaces (having been announced over the intercom), waiting for Mr. Buttons to say I should come up, when a small parade snaked through the front door and stopped not far from me.

There were two huge models, and a blond woman who turned out to be a *Vogue* editor named Cathy McManus, and a striking-looking photographer (he was bony, like Yul Brynner, but with hair) who had a camera on a stand and a black velvet focusing cloth with appliqués on it.

They set up to go to work, and I sat there wondering who they were, and after a few minutes of discussion with the blond woman, the photographer approached me. "Have you ever done any modeling?" he said.

I stared at him, wondering if he was a white slaver.

He repeated his question, and this time I spoke right up. "Huh?" I said.

He told me his name was Clifford Coffin, and he asked if I'd like to come to the *Vogue* studios the following morning. "Does a cat like cream?" I might have countered. "Is the Pope a Catholic?" But I only gulped.

Just then the doorman appeared with the news that I'd been summoned into the Buttons presence. I fled upstairs.

I'd no sooner got inside Mr. Buttons' place than the house phone rang. "It's *Vogue*," Buttons said, looking puzzled. "For you."

I smiled grandly, as though Irving Penn called me everywhere I went, but then I got flustered because Coffin, on the other end, was giving me street numbers and times, while Red and Mrs. Buttons watched me as though considering whether they ought to send for help.

I got back to the office and told Albert I was quitting my job. "They get forty dollars an hour to start," I said.

"To start what?" he said.

But I had no time to explain. I had to go home and go to bed, even though it was only four o'clock. Beauty sleep is everything to us models.

When I walked into the *Vogue* studios the next day, my heart sank. Every girl for miles around was six feet tall, and I was a scant five foot five. I asked myself that Robert Benchley question: "Are you a fire hydrant in a line of trees?" and then pointed out this flaw in my otherwise flawless self to Mr. Coffin, who paid no heed. He was creating. He was going to make

9

something of me. There was no such thing as a too-short high-fashion model (a low-fashion model?). There were only girls who didn't make good because they whined when they should have waxed. "Besides, Mary Jane Whatsis"—a famous high-fashion model—"is only five feet four."

They took off my clothes and escorted me, with a coat over my delicate underthings—excuse me: gommints—into a cab, and thence to an apartment maintained by the illustrator Jon Whitcomb in an East Side pleasure dome called River House. They strapped me with a Turkish towel so I'd be flat-chested, and they stood me up against a piano in a white dress with vegetables on it, and they fastened the dress behind me with clothespins.

They told me to break my ankle. (That meant, I discovered, turning my ankle bone toward the camera, so my feet wouldn't look stiff.)

They combed my hair and powdered my nose between every shot, and there was one boy who did nothing but hold a big silver reflector (like those cardboards used for suntanning) around my chin, while somebody else read a light meter.

There was a woman with a box of jewelry and gloves and other accessories, and she draped me with some of these, while Mr. Coffin and Miss McManus conferred.

They took pictures by the piano and on a bench and out on the terrace, and then we went back to *Vogue* and they took pictures in the studio.

There I got my first glimpse of the instrument known as a model's stand. It's an iron pole, with a seat at the top, which comes up and meets your tail at an angle. It can't be seen in pictures, but you can rest against it while they frame you in great rings of light and discuss your potential.

"See, in the ground glass she looks just like Nuh-*tah*-lee,"

Coffin kept telling Miss McManus, who would obediently look in the ground glass and agree. I didn't know who Nuh-*tah*-lee was, but I also didn't think it was my place to ask. Being a model —a beginner model, anyway—is like being a davenport. You're polished up, slipcovered and moved around, but nobody talks to you.

Still, it was exciting. Visions of the *dolce vita* danced through my head, especially when Coffin phoned some editor about a hair article he was going to illustrate and reeled off the models he wanted, and added casually, "I've just found this new girl. I'd like you to book her too."

Because the Fords' agency was the outfit through which Coffin did most of his booking, he said he wanted me to work out of there. Now, Fords' is an agency that handled mostly high-fashion models, as opposed to agencies that handled American-girl models (toothpaste ads, Coca-Cola ads, etc.) or agencies that handled housewife models ("How can I eat this peach, Charlie? My dentures will slip").

These days, there's so much money in TV that the lines have blurred somewhat, but at that time the Fords' models were almost all very tall, very willowy, with cheekbones like e.e. cummings.

If I'd walked into Fords' off the street, Eileen Ford would have had a good laugh and turned me out again. But since *Vogue* was interested, I heard about Mary Jane Whatsis again. "She's only five feet four and works every minute."

Eileen Ford herself was a small, brown-haired woman, pleasant- but not spectacular-looking, and her husband and partner, Jerry, was a large, handsome ex-model. The first thing Mrs. Ford told me was to lose ten pounds and "always wear a cinch." Since I weighed about eighty pounds right after dinner, and was in constant danger of being mistaken by a hungry dog for a bone

11

he'd buried last week, I was a trifle unstrung.

After the cinch speech, Mrs. Ford picked up a scissors, chopped off four or five of my twelve hairs and said, "Go to Caruso."

Caruso was a hair stylist so chic that if you went to his shop, you could spend two hours getting a hairdo which was guaranteed to last ten minutes. Your hair came out so fine and free and swinging that if you got caught in a wind, you had to go right back and have it done over again, but you looked so great it was worth it. Since I'd grown up in neighborhoods where the housewives had those little anchovy curls set all over their heads—"It should keep good for a week"—Caruso was a revelation.

Maybe you think starting at the top—Coffin, *Vogue*, Fords', Caruso—automatically leads to fooling around with millionaires in Brigitte Bardot's villa at Saint-Tropez.

Forget it.

(Though that editor, Cathy McManus, married a marquis or a count or a duke, and now lives in Italy as Catherine di Montezemolo.)

But I never even got to see those pictures Coffin took.

I'd been passion's plaything, used up, thrown aside, a whim to while away a summer's day. What had happened? I asked myself. Nuh-*tah*-lee in the ground glass, chopped liver in the developer? Could it be?

And I'd quit my job, and was too ashamed to go ask for it back. As it turned out, all I had to do was drop the magic names of *Vogue* and Coffin—"He discovered me," I'd murmur shyly— and that got me other modeling jobs. I was no Jean Shrimpton, but I made some money. And I earned it, too, shivering on the beach at Montauk in bathing suits in March (I'd been ignorant of the fact that magazines have to work way ahead), sweltering in skunk coats in August.

12

Still, I wasn't really any good. The trick in modeling is to believe you're gorgeous, to bloom, so to speak, for the camera. You have to have a fat ego. As a model I had no ego at all, and I worried night and day. Here they were, paying me all this money, and what if the pictures turned out terrible? It got so I couldn't sleep, for fear I was putting some magazine out of business. It was time, I decided, to become a movie star. . . .

3

How to Become a Movie Star

Now I'll tell everybody how to become a movie star. You just sit around in your apartment for about twenty years, and then this guy comes in with a contract.

Honest. I wouldn't lie about such a serious subject.

The way it began, I had a friend named Bert Stern. We used to compare our humble beginnings. My grandmother lived in Brooklyn and spoke in mottoes like "Cleansiness is next to godness," "Own praise don't go a great ways" and "Weep and you sleep alone"; Bert's mother lived in Brooklyn and referred to the dog as "the Irish settler," so there was a bond between us. We spent a good deal of our time together trying to decide which forks to use if we were invited to dinner by the great. We had every intention of hobnobbing with the great; neither of us cared to remain shabby or obscure.

To be sure, Bert had scarcely finished high school, but I hadn't gone to Harvard myself, and we assumed that such polish as we needed we'd scrounge along the way. Bert had worked in the mailroom at *Look* magazine, where he'd met another ambitious kid named Stanley Kubrick, and after that he'd gone to a short-lived publication called *Flair*, and still later he'd been art director of something known as *Fashion and Travel*, and then he'd turned to photography, and then he'd got sent away to the Korean War.

All the time he was in Korea, I only heard from Bert once. He

14

wrote me a card which said Korean whiskey is very good. It will *(a)* blind you, *(b)* kill you or *(c)* blind you and kill you.

When he returned from the Orient, Bert came to visit me. I was hiding in a little place I had in the Village. I was living there quite happily, because I never went out in the street. I had various friends who looked after me; they brought in groceries, took out cleaning, and I didn't think there was anything odd about it. To pay the rent I was modeling some (which wasn't easy, since I tended to cover my face with my hands as soon as the photographer looked into the camera), but when I wasn't working I was right there in that apartment.

So this night Bert came over, he brought Stanley Kubrick with him. Kubrick had made two films, a short called *The Day of the Fight*, about a Golden Gloves champion named Walter Cartier, and a feature called *Fear and Desire*. All I remember about *Fear and Desire* was that a girl was tied to a tree, and later on she drank water out of a soldier's hand. All the soldiers were on both sides. Something like that.

Anyhow, Stanley was looking for an actress to play the lead in his new movie, the script of which was bulging out his pocket.

Bert made the introductions, and I handled the scene with my usual finesse. I went and crouched behind a television set in the corner.

It made an impression on Kubrick, all right. "Your friend's pretty," he said to Bert, "but she's a little odd."

Since I wouldn't come out, they finally went away, after which I reviled myself. "Lowlife! Coward! Why don't you behave like a clean-limbed American girl?" I didn't answer that at all. I looked haughty, and stayed down there behind the television set.

Next day, Kubrick appeared at my door, without Bert. He said he'd like me to read for him, and he showed me a soliloquy

15

which went on for about six minutes, with the heroine's explaining her incestuous feelings for her father, her guilt about the death of her sister, her idea of expiation—living in a crummy place with toast all over the floor, though she'd only recently dwelt in marble halls on Long Island—and I said, "I can't do it."

Stanley was patient. "Make us some coffee," he said, "and we'll talk."

An hour or so later, he thrust the script at me again. This time I did the six-minute soliloquy in three and a half minutes flat. He was enraptured. "You're going to be a great star," he said. It was like a Betty Grable movie, the scene where Betty takes off her glasses and she's beautiful.

Stanley started talking about contracts, and I collapsed again. "But my voice is funny," I said. (I have what Frank Loesser, if I may name-drop for a moment, called "a little-boy voice." People are always getting me on the phone and saying, "Sonny, let me talk to your father.")

Stanley said he loved my voice, it would become famous, kids would imitate it the way they did Marlon Brando's.

I signed the contract.

All the actors in that picture were working on what is called "deferral." I think it's illegal. It means you get paid a certain percentage of your salary every week, and the rest out of profits. If any. For instance, Frank Silvera, who played the villain, was getting $1,000 a week on paper, and drawing $100. I was contracted for $650, and took home what was left out of $65 after taxes.

It didn't matter to me. I would have paid Stanley. Here it was, my first acting job, and I was starring in a movie.

Now Stanley said he wanted me to have long hair. I had, thanks to Eileen Ford, short hair and, thanks to nature, fine hair. We knew it wasn't going to grow in, long and luxuriant, before

16

shooting started, so we decided on a wig, and I set off for a theatrical wigmaker on Forty-fourth Street.

In 1955 wigs weren't so commonplace. That is, just regular-people wigs, nice plain straight hair such as an ordinary starlet might wear while hoping to attract Paul Newman.

In Hollywood the studios used to equip you if God hadn't. Betty Garrett once told me a story about the late Judy Holliday which illustrates this point. Judy Holliday had been signed for a picture, and had gone out to meet the head of the studio, who was a bit of a lecher. He would run off a new player's test right before he went in to view that new player in the flesh. It stimulated his imagination. Anyhow, Miss Holliday was taken over by the studio publicity people, who wanted her to put her best foot forward, not to mention all her other best features, and they marched her into makeup and added eyelashes and rouge, and then they took her into wardrobe and glued a tight black dress onto her and rounded out the picture with large foam-rubber falsies.

Thus furnished, she was sent into an office the size of Rhode Island to await the great man's appearance. Nervously she walked across the carpet and sat down on a couch behind a vast marble-topped coffee table.

The magnate came in, strewing bottle caps before him, as was his habit, then flicking them out of his way with a polo mallet. He made a dive for Miss Holliday across the marble table and came up, astonished, with a foam-rubber pad in his hand.

Into the embarrassed silence Judy spoke. "It's all right, Mr. Soandso," she said kindly. "It belongs to you."

Nothing that exciting happened to me on Forty-fourth Street. The wigmaker showed me a white job with powdered curls fore and aft, suitable for playing Louis XIV (or his uncles and his cousins and his aunts), and when I whimpered no, he showed me a fine stiff black Cleopatra headdress, and when I still whimpered no, he turned on his heel. "Honey," he said, "send the teacher in."

Some way to talk to a movie star, I thought, and went back downtown.

We spent a year on that movie, mostly in alleys with big signs that said NO TOILET, and on rooftops and city streets and deserted warehouses, and before it was done I was cold and tired and sick of it, with it, from it. But the first day, the day I reported for work, I nearly died of happiness.

I remember waking up, and the mail was there, and I had a letter from my sister (who'd read that you always wished people luck when they started a picture, and who was doing for me what she believed so many had done for Lana Turner).

I skipped through Washington Square Park on my way to the studio on Third Street, and the sun was shining, and the chess players were playing, and the junkies hadn't yet inherited the benches, and I was in my blue jeans, on my way to rule the world.

I remember, too, moving around the set that was my room, the room where the girl I was playing was supposed to live. I touched every prop, every dish, every bobby pin. I listened to the musical powder box. I went and put my hands against the walls. And I thought, Nothing will ever be this good again.

I suppose beginnings are exciting because nothing's been spoiled yet; you still have the dream whole.

A year or so later, I saw *Roman Holiday* with Audrey Hepburn, and I realized there were first breaks and first breaks. There was a girl being given her baptism by silver screen, and it wasn't in any alley with a NO TOILET sign. The director had set her, like a jewel, into the middle of beautiful Rome, with beautiful clothes and beautiful Gregory Peck, and it made me sick.

I was to learn that this kind of sickness was by no means unique to me; all actresses suffer from it. Not long ago I met Maureen O'Hara, and she confessed she'd always been jealous of Jennifer Jones. "When she was married to Selznick," Miss O'Hara said of Miss Jones, "they'd shoot a scene forty times, and he'd look at all the film and print the stuff she looked best in. Whenever *I* made a picture, if the horse didn't you-know-what in the middle of the shot, it was a take!"

I now comfort myself with the thought that there's probably someone who makes Audrey Hepburn sick. Greta Garbo. Or Tuesday Weld.

Anyhow, *Killer's Kiss*, the movie I made for Kubrick, had quite a vogue among intellectuals. It was so bleak they all took it for part of the new wave, and I got a letter from some fellows who wanted to start a fan club for me at Princeton.

I didn't let them.

I never let anybody do anything.

I was still so shy that, after the movie came out, newspaper people would call and ask to speak to me, and I would whisper that I didn't do interviews, and then they'd call Kubrick, furious. "Who's that kid think she is, Bette Davis?" they would ask, and Stanley would tell them yes.

At the time he was living off the unemployment checks of a dancer named Ruth Sobotka (who later became his second wife, and who still later became his second ex-wife), and since Stanley and Ruth were in love, there was a whole ballet sequence set into the movie.

The Theatre de Lys in Greenwich Village was hired for a week, and Ruth went down there and pirouetted and hopped around *en pointe*, and then this one-person ballet was shown on the screen, while my voice droned on about what a gorgeous, terrific, noble creature my dead sister had been. My dead sister the dancer.

Actually, it wasn't my voice that droned on; it was the voice of a radio actress named Peggy Lobbin. *Killer's Kiss* used dubbed sound, and I was against it. I felt sure Duse wouldn't have dubbed. I was equally sure that *no* great talent could have borne to stand in that little studio and stare at himself on the screen and try to fit words, off what's called a loop script, into his own mouth, over and over again, until the mechanicalness of the process drove him mad.

Not that I didn't try. For eight hours I tried, and then I threw my loop script on the floor and went to Florida.

In case anybody doesn't know what dubbing is, I'll attempt, out of my own sketchy knowledge, to explain. Ordinarily movies are shot with what's called synchronized sound. The film and the sound track all roll together, and except for certain outdoor scenes, the dialogue comes right along with the picture.

Nowadays a lot of synchronous sound is shot out of doors, too, moviemakers having been wised up that planes *do* fly over houses, and dogs *do* bark in the streets, and it isn't going to bother viewers if some of the natural noises of the world aren't filtered out.

But for certain action shots, and certain location shots, it's necessary to dub. You can't always get a horse close enough to the mike so you can hear what his rider is saying.

And dubbing is the torture I describe. They project the scene over and over for you, and you read the words that you've said, live, over and over, until those words are quite, quite dead.

In my opinion. Because there's a way a voice is colored just by the body's bending, or turning, or stretching, that doesn't exist in dubbing. Dubbing's one-level sound, all stale, flat and unprofitable, if you ask me. Which nobody has.

The dubbing crisis came at the end of it all, though, and in the beginning the movie was one long party. I got a crush on the cameraman and went to work every day, whether I was called or not, and helped lug equipment to the roof of whatever building the fellows were tearing across at the time. Stanley looked up one morning and made a directorial pronouncement. "Chris is a good actress," he said. "She carries a lot."

Now that he's so famous, what with having made *2001: A Space Odyssey* and *Clockwork Orange,* I try to think if I could have spotted his incipient genius. My sister Linda says no, and offers as proof some letters I sent her during the shooting of *Killer's Kiss.* Here are a couple of examples:

Darling girl,

Thank you for the good wishes, though of course I don't need them. After all, I'm in the hands of a lunatic who looks fully seventeen years old, has black hair that grows down over his neck, quotes widely from Henry Miller—the dirty parts—and takes time out from shooting to discuss with his girl friend the sex habits of some canaries who are living in her apartment.

There's a still man (that's a man who shoots non-moving pictures) who's come to inhabit my armpit; no matter what I'm doing, or how I'm dressed, he's always there looking up at me with his beady little lens. Making a movie is boring. You spend hours and hours waiting for somebody to screw in a light bulb, and then when you get ready to really do a scene, sob, cry, scream, they stop you in the middle and hold a tape measure to the end of your nose, and draw chalk marks around your shoes, and otherwise inhibit you. I don't know how Jean-Louis Barrault does it.

Stanley's a fascinating character. He thinks movies should

21

move, with a minimum of dialogue, and he's all for sex and sadism. Talks about Mickey Spillane, and how the public eats it up. He's also totally sure of himself. Knows where he's going, how he's going to get there, and who's going to pick up the tab for the trip. He drove me home the other night, after a huge scene on the set—scene by stagehands, not actors—in which everybody complained of cold, tiredness, lack of funds, and then Frank Silvera said there was an off-Broadway play he could be doing right this minute, or at least be reading for, if he didn't have to stay down here in the gutter with the rest of us. And Stanley listened to the whole thing, then very sweetly told everybody to take off, we were finished for the day. After we got in the car, I asked him how he could be so patient, and he grinned. "Baby, nobody's going to get anything out of this movie but me."

Do you think it's possible?

Love, C

Dear baby linder lindia liniment (can you say lemon liniment three times fast?), I have been dancing in a dance hall in a black satin dress with this and that make-believe sailor, and somewhere along the line, I've hurt the feelings of one of the guys who's playing a bouncer. Stanley was defending me against this fellow's attack, and I chanced to hear the end of the dialogue.

"Yeah, Chris is okay," the fellow finally said. "It's just her personality stinks."

This is the same actor who goes to the rushes every night along with Stanley and me. You can't pay anybody else to come. Actor-bouncer sits there admiring his catlike grace. "Cheez, looka dat, I move like a pant-er."

We have shot a bunch of endings for this plate of hash, and by now I don't know if I'm a bad guy or a good guy. There's one version where I kill the villain, there's another version where I try to seduce him, there's been more killing and resurrection than you'll find in the Bible. The other day I was playing a love scene with a guy named Jamie Smith (he told me he would never

22

go to Strasberg, he doesn't believe in *that kind* of acting) when, in the middle of a kiss, he suddenly reached up and grabbed my left chest very firmly, as the camera ground away. I leaped to my feet screaming and calling Jamie and Stanley bad names (they'd clearly set the whole thing up behind my back) and Stanley gave me the foreign markets lecture.

It goes, "No, darling, we'd never show it that way in this country, but in Europe, everybody's broad-minded."

"Bully for Europe," I said, "but I'm narrow-minded, and I want you to burn that film."

Naturally, many promises were made, and I went home crying, with the cameraman following me downstairs, earnestly explaining that "they" did feel different about things in Europe, especially the Germans and the French. How the Chinese respond, I don't know. I guess I could ask Daddy. I called him the other night, and he said he was the houseboy. "Oh, Chin?" I asked. "No," he told me. "Double Chin."

Maybe I'm just tired, but I'm beginning to suspect that if I follow this particular rainbow which has been stretched across my small horizon, I am going to find a pot at the end of it, all right, but what it will be filled with isn't gold.

Your own precious baby star,

C

4

Letter to My Sister, or How, When I Asked This Guy at the Ad Agency What He Was Doing Now, He Said, "I'm Working with Strasberg, Trying to Expose Myself"

Pigling o' mine,

(in Rome, the hotel had roast pigling on the menu, also pumpking soup with tapioca), you ask me about Strasberg, and should your friend go to him, and if he's *really* the guru I've cracked him up to be, and I feel the breath of your doubt warming the back of my neck.

The discussion about Method acting is so boring by now. Good actors have always used it. Half the time they haven't known they were using it and scorned the mere suggestion. Paul McGrath was in *Command Decision* with Paul Kelly, and every night, during one scene, Kelly would cry real tears. It was so remarkable, the tears coursing down that granite face, and so moving, and so dependable, that Paul McGrath got curious. He went to Kelly. "Listen," he said, "how do you manage to do that every single night? Do you have a technique?"

And Kelly looked at McGrath as if McGrath had accused him of wearing a tutu down Third Avenue. "You mean that Method crap?" he said. "Hell, no."

After a minute he added, "I just think about the time my mother died, out in Brooklyn."

That's Method.

I think your buddy could find out what she wants to know by reading Stanislavski. But as for going to Lee, it seems to me unthinkable to live in this country at a time when he's teaching and pass up the chance to study with him.

If I'd been around when Edmund Kean or Duse was acting, wild horses couldn't have kept me from going to find out what the fuss was about, and I don't think anyone but Lee can really convey what Lee does.

Including me. But since your friend apparently wants a serious answer, I'll try to say what I believe.

To begin, Strasberg can't make an actor, any more than journalism schools can make writers. The raw material comes from nature. Ideally it's a combination of sensitivity and guts and imagination and a skin thin enough so you can respond easily, and thick enough so you don't bleed to death every time you're rejected.

Given these blessings, and a few others—it's good to have relatives in high places, it's better to look like the young Elizabeth Taylor—you can take your equipment to Lee, and he'll show you how to get the most out of it.

He says technique is a crutch. If you're working well, if you're inspired by the scene, you don't need it. But there are nights when one isn't inspired, and actors aren't in a business that permits them to go out and make a curtain speech: "Please, I don't feel it, will you come back tomorrow?" The audience is entitled to the actor's best every single night. So technique comes to his rescue when he's dull, tired or bored.

I used to get sick of hearing that everybody Lee teaches mumbles. And scratches. I once heard the late Helen Menken

25

deploring "ahss-scratching Actors Studio actors," but assuming some guys itch, is that Lee's fault?

I remember reading how foolish it was to talk about a *New Yorker* "school" of writing, when that magazine had printed talents so diverse as Benchley, O'Hara, Perelman, Parker, Lardner, Gibbs, Salinger, Updike, Cheever, yet the careless and the glib lumped them all together.

It's the same with the Actors Studio. Kim Stanley, Julie Harris, Brando, Eli Wallach, Maureen Stapleton—the ones considered the cream of a generation ago—all worked with Lee, and they're all good actors, some better than others, depending on your taste, but surely as different in flavor one from another as olives are from radishes, or bass drums are from flutes.

What Lee tries to do is help free the "you of you," as the kid in *Member of the Wedding* called it.

The other thing that's never mentioned (because Lee's a high priest and all this reverence and mystery surrounds him) is that Lee's funny. Very funny, and very plain. He doesn't have an elaborate language, the way so many acting teachers do. He doesn't talk about objectives and obstacles and beats and spines and justifications. He has two kinds of exercises; they are sense memories and emotional (or affective) memories.

Even these are really two halves of the same thing, since you reach your emotions through your senses. That is, a particular piece of music can induce in you a particular mood, the same way that the smell of leaves burning may bring back something that happened to you on a fall day long ago. Sense memories are powerful, so the even more powerful affective memories aren't necessary for any but peak moments in a play.

"An actor's actual experiences condition him," Lee says. "If he has six or a dozen keys, it's enough. These motors are used for strong (shock) emotions, when something has to happen *this*

26

moment, as though it had never happened before. For less violent things, sensory memory will generally do."

When kids start working on the Method, they want to have reasons for everything. Direct a guy to walk across the stage, and he says, Why? Why would the character I'm playing do that? What's my motivation?

Lee cuts through the pretentiousness. "If I'm the boss, and I say walk across the stage, walk across the stage. You don't need a reason. You're getting paid is the reason. And you'll get fired if you don't is the other reason. But why make such a problem? In life, people walk across the room and they don't have a reason. That's an easy thing to do. If I tell you to do something hard, that's another story. To smash somebody, to get hysterical —for these you may need help. If somebody asks for a penny, give it to him. A thousand dollars is different. If I ask an actor to sit down, go and sit down. You don't need motivation. Who the hell cares?"

Nobody can be convinced—nobody who doesn't know him— that Lee says anything that direct. It doesn't sound metaphysical enough to satisfy his detractors.

He has a way of speaking which is close to the way a child speaks, fresh, often lyrical. In single sentences he's summed up complicated acting problems, and I've watched him do it in scene after scene after scene, never cheating or holding back no matter how tired or personally distracted he may have been. Always he gave full value, and then some.

You want examples? Here:

To a girl who was all emotion, no technique, he said, "Blood without flesh and bones only spills."

To a boy who was all technique, no logic, he said, "Nothing we do technically has value unless it is directed to a purpose; climbing mountains to prove you're limber is pointless unless

27

the actor's playing Romeo and has to scale walls."

To a self-conscious man trying to do a sense memory of holding an egg: "You behave as though you were an egg yourself."

To a couple who'd worked on only half the elements in a scene: "I ask for bread and butter. You give me bread and tell me butter's in the icebox. So now I've got bread and butter? No. Besides feeling and thought, everything must have a specific reality."

He told us we had to learn about ourselves, because you can imagine you are acting beautifully and from out front it comes across wrong. "Some people, when they think about love, it looks like a stomachache. Some people, when they think about food, it looks like love. On a piano you can play with your elbows; on a violin, not. Each person is an instrument with varied colors; he must know himself. A literal parallel doesn't always work onstage."

People who put on acts for Strasberg got short shrift. You couldn't con him. Tell him, expecting he'll find it enchanting, that you love to walk in the rain, and a glint appears in his eye. "You'd make a good mailman."

One of the first classes I went to, there was a girl doing a sense memory of standing on a hill with the wind blowing through her hair.

She posed up on the stage for a while, then looked stricken. "I can't, I can't. . . ."

Lee was calm. "You can't what, dolling?"

"I can't feel the wind," she said. "It's gone. . . ."

Lee rubbed his nose. It's his most famous gesture. "Dolling, if I'm playing the piano with a symphony orchestra and my pants fall down, I have to go right on playing the piano. Sure I hope I'll get a minute and I'll pull up my pants, but I can't just stop in the middle."

28

He was telling her that she had to keep her concentration going, and whatever she was working for would eventually come back to her, but the vividness of his examples stayed in your head long after the pomposities of other directors were forgotten.

He was hardest on people he expected most of. (With beginners he was endlessly patient, even letting them lecture him for a while. Eventually he'd get tired of this, and say to some argumentative clod, "Look, did you come to study with me, or did I come to study with you?") I've seen an actress in such an excess of emotion that she'd run offstage, unable to finish a scene, and instead of complimenting her on the fullness of her feeling, Lee was furious. "Without will," he said sternly, "sensitivity is of no value."

Conversely, when he gave you a medal, you remembered that too. A boy and a girl did a scene from an old drama called *Roadside*, and Lee was knocked out. "Arthur Hopkins staked his life and reputation twice on this play, and nobody knew why. I didn't either. Now I do, and it's because of something you people have done, with your honesty and simplicity."

If he paid you a particularly generous tribute, everybody in class suddenly wanted to do scenes with you.

I'm going on and on like this, and I don't know if I'm telling your friend the stuff she's worried about. Maybe all she really wanted to know was that she should write Lee for an appointment, and that his secretary would set up an interview and tell her what his rates are. Or maybe she wanted to know where he holds his classes. (When I went to him, more than fifteen years ago, it was simpler. You approached him and said you'd like to study with him, and he looked you over and said okay, or else he didn't say okay. And he taught in crummy studios with hard seats, and little raised platforms for stages, and you brought

29

your own props and you paid him less than you should have because, in the end, he loved actors and could hardly stand to charge them.)

He makes it all seem simple.

He tells you tension is just misplaced energy. Like electricity, which can light up the room or electrocute you, depending on how you use it, energy has to be directed properly. "If you say to a child, 'Don't cry,' it won't work, but you can channel his ideas in another direction. Legitimate questions engender legitimate concentration, not fake concentration. For instance, I've got to concentrate on that chair. Stare at it and all that happens is my neck gets stiff. But suppose I start to think, How much does a chair like that cost? How wide across is it? How tall?"

Since tension is the actor's cross, Lee comes back to it again and again. "Mental effort is *impeded* by tension, physical effort is *deformed* by tension. Say you're tense, and somebody tells you to jump. You can jump, even if peculiarly, and the jump will relax you. But if somebody tells you to multiply thirty-five by thirty-five, the mind simply will not go."

I took notes only for the first five or six classes, when it was all new to me, yet even out of those few sessions gold was gleanable.

"If the object is real, if you can create the love, the desire, the need, then your hands will know, your body will know."

"Don't try to make yourself a vessel of expression. Work specifically."

"You stop yourself from doing something because you're afraid you won't do it well. Make the effort and you'll get fifteen results."

"Some people are natural, but not real."

30

"If you have pain, and you do something with your hands, some of the pain goes into your hands, even if you hold a nice object in your hands."

"It's what we do that conditions how we speak, not how we speak that conditions what we do."

"The movies were created so that under socially accepted and controlled circumstances you could live other people's lives."

"Do not use your voice apologetically."

"Do not permit your mind to limp."

"Do not make up thoughts and meanings which are not logical."

"Follow through with what you tell yourself. Be horrible, if necessary, but *do* what you set out to *do.*"

That ought to give your friend an idea of whether or not the great man is for her. But what I'm not able to convey is a kind of magic Lee has. He is in love with the theatre ("The theatre is my church") and the history of the theatre, and the traditions of the theatre, and the great works of the theatre, and he can communicate his passion, and make you feel proud to be an actor, instead of feeling the usual way, which is a little embarrassed and a good deal too needy.

When he tells you what should go into a scene, the play seems to happen before your eyes. After a bit from *Anna Christie,* in which the actress wasn't bad, but she wasn't really good either, Lee explained why. "The lines have meaning only in relation to something that has happened. When the curtain goes up, you must believe in the culmination of some whole thing that has gone before. The tiredness of the woman, the hope, though she's hopeless. Do not think of what's coming out; it's what propels the coming out. The actress here used her discomfort

31

so she could talk. No. Use it so you *cannot* talk. Then it would come out like Anna. Fog, loneliness, past, seeking, seeking, like a dog who's been beaten, and shies if you raise an arm. Then she finds what she wants, but it's no use because of her past. And she sits for two days, steeping in this."

That's what Stanislavski called "given circumstances"— what's gone before which makes the scene you're about to play inevitable.

Sometimes, looking back, I find Lee almost too right, his insights so sharp there's a spookiness to them.

A student had done a scene from *The Seven Year Itch*, and the scene hadn't played funny. Lee dissected the character she was attempting. "There's only one thing a girl like the *Seven Year Itch* girl is made for. She always flirts, even if only with the grocery man. She's a woman. Also naïve. That girl would hover, nuzzle, stand too close. When she appears at the door, it's as if for an assignation, even though she's just coming for a plant. In life, this kind of girl tells people her troubles and they don't listen. *She's* got troubles? One man, another man, what difference does it make? Then you read in the paper a girl like that's taken an overdose of sleeping pills."

This was before Marilyn Monroe, who played *The Seven Year Itch* in the movies, ever came to Lee to study.

I'll quit now. I'm afraid this sounds too serious, too dreary, too everything that Lee is not. But tell your friend to go to the source, and she won't regret it.

You never know what's going to happen in a Strasberg class, so it's always entertaining, even if you don't get to work. A new girl rose one day and did her first exercise, and she began to weep and sniffle, and when it was over, Lee said fine, what was it.

"Sunshine," said the new girl.

32

"Sunshine?" said Lee. "Sunshine makes you cry?"

"Like it bugs me," said the new girl.

Your loving relative, Eleanora

P.S. Method types say if you've ever stalked a mosquito, you can play Othello. And if you believe that, I'll tell you another.

5

Fortune and Men's Eyes

*Half the fun of being an actor is getting away from
your own disgusting self.*

Richard Burton

Richard Burton didn't say that to me; he said it to a reporter.
He's never spoken to me. He's never even knocked me down
and broken my camera. But I collect the sayings of the great
against the time when I achieve greatness. I want to know how
to behave on the day a columnist accosts me, hoping for a
printable witticism.

I've got a few *mots* planned, if I can *juste* bring them off. Say
Earl Wilson and I (hereinafter referred to as Big Star) meet on
the street outside of an exotic delicatessen which features
chocolate-covered grasshoppers and canned rattlesnake meat.
It will go like this:

Earl: "Did you ever eat rattlesnake?"

B.S.: "Sure."

Earl: "Howcome?"

B.S. (with a warm chuckle): "It was him or me."

But how do you get one of those conversations started? What
if he only says, Nice day, ain't it? and keeps right on going. What
if he doesn't say anything at all? It certainly isn't dignified to
chase him up the block, sables flapping.

Okay; if he's gonna be like that, I'll ignore him. I'll give my all to Sidney Skolsky, who will tintype me for posterity. After he's established what I sleep in (a laundry bag with a hole cut out for my head and a picture of a pilgrim on the front) and what I eat for breakfast (snake meat—I want to fit that joke in somewhere), he will get down to serious business.

Sid: "If you had it to do over again, what would you change?"

B.S. (with a mad twinkle): "My underwear!"

Whenever I tell my husband about this campaign that will result in my being internationally recognized as a wit, he says, "Well, you're half right, anyway," and other mean remarks he learned in grammar school, but I know that true greatness is impervious to slurs.

Picture me crossing swords with another actor, as we indulge in a bit of horseplay between takes (crossing horses with another actor, as we indulge in a bit of swordplay between takes?). "I played Othello," he'll brag. "Who won?" I'll shoot back, quick as a wink.

I had a retort which would have been guaranteed to earn me space in *The Daily Worker* (somebody says, "The meek shall inherit the earth," and I mutter, "Yeah, mouthfuls of it") but *The Daily Worker* went out of business, and I've still got a neat one for *Travel & Leisure*.

The *T & L* gag requires setting up, but I know how to do it. There'll be a splendid shipboard party in honor of myself, on the eve of a European sailing. Everywhere will be freeloading journalists, photographers, publicity men, hanging on my words and deeds. A stranger's eyes meet mine across the Taittinger brut. "I'm going to Greece," says the stranger.

"I'm running to fat myself, friend," I'll retort.

This stuff all comes to me in the middle of the night, when I'm not under pressure—though to tell the truth, *Time* magazine hasn't been knocking my door down in the daytime either

—but so far, on my very occasional interviews, I haven't been able to put any of my ideas to work.

For a while, I was getting a bit of a reputation for being a fascinating interviewee because I said nothing at all. Absolutely nothing. It was okay on television, where audiences could see I was still breathing, but radio listeners must have had the nagging feeling that somebody was introduced back there and then took poison.

In San Francisco I once "guested" on the Gypsy Rose Lee show, where my silence wasn't too noticeable (Gypsy talked so much you'd have had to punch her in the mouth to get a word in edgewise), but sometimes it was worse than that.

I went on a TV show in Las Vegas where I *did* talk, but my conversation wasn't picked up and quoted anywhere.

What happened was a lady M.C. introduced me as lovely Edith Kane (one of my acting names is Irene Kane, not exactly a household word but not Edith either) and I said my name wasn't Edith. After talking to other guests, who sang and had big busts, the M.C. came back to me and said, "Well, Edith dear, how's it going?" and I said my name wasn't Edith again. I must have said it three or four times in all, but there's plenty of sour grapes-ers who don't think that's much to brag about.

When confronted by a direct question (example: "How old are you?") I tend to stammer, "Gee, uh, I don't know" (which isn't so dumb if you're an actress), but ordinarily I hold my tongue, the way I was brought up to do, and am God's dullest copy.

The one time I ever made anyone even smile on an interview show, it was unintentional. A woman named Bea Kalmus was conducting a late-night radio forum from a midtown New York restaurant, at a time when I was working at the Paper Mill

Playhouse in New Jersey and the Paper Mill's publicity people
were covering any local programs that might bring business
their way. So, over my fervent objections, they sent me and the
juvenile who was playing opposite me to visit Bea Kalmus.

My cohort and I were the lowliest, least celebrated, most
unknown parties to the felony, and we sat at a table and
watched most of the show before we were ever brought on.
First there was an actress named Jessie Royce Landis, who
talked about Alfred Hitchcock, and how good he'd been to her,
and then there was George C. Scott, who discussed *The Hustler*.
By the time the juvenile and I went on, it was pretty late, but
I kept telling myself to speak clearly, say what the play was, say
who was starring in it (Arthur Treacher was starring in it), say
how funny it was and how much audiences loved it, and how
there were still some seats available.

To myself, I said all this. But at least I had it in mind. I knew
what I was there for.

Not so my partner. The hell with plugging a summer-stock
turkey, he must have thought, and proceeded to try and curry
favor with George C. Scott (who was by then sitting at the bar
watching *us*). That juvenile told Bea Kalmus that George C.
Scott was his idol, that he preferred him to Laurence Olivier,
that he wished he was fit to kiss the hem of George C. Scott's
robes, that he considered George C. Scott's Richard III to be the
definitive performance of the age.

Twenty minutes later, Miss Kalmus turned to me. "You," she
said accusingly, "haven't uttered a single word." "I never saw
George C. Scott play Richard III," I blurted. It made George C.
Scott fall off the barstool laughing, but I really wasn't trying to
be smart.

Later on, Mr. Scott went up to the juvenile who so admired

him, and thrust a thumb in my direction. "What's she like?"

The juvenile shook his head contemptuously. "She's just what you see there!" he said.

But someday there'll be more to me than meets the eye. I know it. Because for years I've been studying my collection of movie stars' sayings, and getting into the rhythm of how they do it.

My collection goes all the way back to when movie stars were really movie stars, and Kim Novak was dating Colonel Rafael Trujillo. I chose Kim for one of my mentors because she was a wizard at fielding embarrassing questions.

She'd given her heart—or some part of it—to this Ramfils cat (whose daddy had owned the Dominican Republic) and in return she'd got a shiny new automobile, her carved initials entwined with his on a sturdy oak tree and the assurance that she came first with him. Or maybe it was sixth or seventh, right after some of his children.

It was pretty much of an idyll, you might say, until a bigot from the press approached Kim with a mean look (the bigot had the mean look; Kim looked lovely). "Gee, Kim," said the bigot, "but this guy to whom you've given your heart—or some part of it—is a dirty would-be dictator."

Kim said Ramfils was nothing of the kind. And he wasn't going to be, either. "Or if he is, he will be a dictator who is loved by his people."

Kim said the reason she hadn't married Ramfils was these selfsame "people." Deep in her heart—or some part of it—"I always had the feeling any marriage with him would be a triangle. Him, me and the people. It made me hesitate."

That's star talk.

Rita Hayworth's another star who knew how to avoid sounding run-of-the-mill. When she found herself at the altar for the fifth time, she said, "My first four marriages seem now to have been mistakes." (I know how she felt. Sometimes I think my whole life has been a mistake.) Three years later, divorcing fifth mate James Hill, Rita was forced to testify, "He said I was not a nice woman in too loud a voice."

I submit that you could have spotted Rita for a princess just by those little things that upset her. Not a nice woman indeed! Imagine if the guy had said, "You lookin' for a fat lip?" or "How would you like a knuckle sangwitch?" which is more or less what I hear in my circle. It's possible I've been held back by my circle. (I prefer not to mention my circle by name, because if I do he'll give me a fat lip and a knuckle sangwitch.)

Sometimes a star can come off good in the public prints if he or she talks about other stars. When I'm not shaking 'em up with my clever ripostes ("I've been to see the Lunts." "In what?" "In their apartment.") I figure to do a decent amount of reminiscing about George Arliss, because I read his biography in English class, and he must have been one tony actor. Unfortunately, the only anecdote I remember from his biography isn't about him.

It concerns Mrs. Patrick Campbell.

It seems there was a young actor who thought that during the rehearsals of a particular play Mrs. Campbell was sitting out front rudely chortling. So he sent around a note asking if Mrs. Campbell would please refrain from laughing at him in the theatre. And she sent back a note saying she never laughed at him in the theatre; she always waited till she got home.

Anyhow, I remember the Mrs. Campbell anecdote because I used it in book reports all the way through high school; it saved my reading any other book on the "required" list. Even in those days I couldn't remember too much about George Arliss, but I can always say I'm sure he was kind.

Kindness used to be the biggest thing in star interviews, back when stars were really stars. Right after a lady star said she didn't care if the man she married was handsome or rich or could tell you-know-what from Shinola, just so he had a sense of humor, she'd also ring in a few words about kindness.

In case you think I'm full of—uh—Shinola, I've got examples.

Dorothy Provine is in my collection, talking about Frank Sinatra. "He's kind," she said, "to everyone he likes."

Marilyn Maxwell gave *her* kindness medal to Rock Hudson. "I think Rock is the kindest man I've ever known."

But Mia Farrow was my last idol, and she didn't even bother about kindness. She told it like it was.

Nobody in Hollywood scared Mia a bit, and it only took her one off-Broadway job before she hit the big time. Since nobody saw the off-Broadway job, I contend it was her guts and her way with the press that really paid off.

"I'm a butterfly," she told everybody. "I have to be free. You can't clamp your hands over a butterfly; when you open them again, you will find only crumpled wings."

That's guts, isn't it? I might *think* of saying I was a butterfly, but visions of horselaughs would dance through my head, and cries of "Banan-er oil!" would ring in my ears, and I'd never do it. Which is why I'm here, and she's mucking around Buckingham Palace with André Previn and the kids.

Mia wasn't humble either, a virtue I've discovered to be highly overrated. About a minute after she came to Hollywood, she was ushered into Paul Monash's office—he produced *Peyton Place*—and the two talked for half an hour, and then Mia came out and told her agent, "He's rather a sad little man, but I think I brought him some happiness."

Monash must have thought so too.

Mia talked freely about how human and vulnerable she was. "Because I feel so deeply, I know I'm bound to get hurt, but when I'm hurt I'll do the only thing possible. I'll pick up the shattered pieces of myself and paste them back together with the moisture from my tears."

Some cynics thought there was a soupçon of paranoia mixed in with her straightforward girlishness—she was alarmed lest anyone try and "stomp" on her, and she planned a garden in which she would "wear long black boots so the snakes can't bite me; the world is full of them, you know"—but it made better copy than "What's your name?" "Puddin' 'n' tane. Ask me again and I'll tell you the same," which is the way *my* past encounters had begun, so I started studying Mia too. Mia, Rita, Kim.

I guess by now you see how I'm going to do it. Handle myself and my famousness, that is. I'm going to be ready for it when it comes. I'm going to be prepared. I'm going to be like Earl Long, that stout-hearted ex-governor of Louisiana, who cited preparedness as the reason why he should be given a fourth term in the state house instead of a spell in the booby hatch. "I have the experience to be governor!" he cried. "I know how to shoot craps! I know how to play poker! I know how to get in and out of the Baptist church!"

Well, I have the experience to be a star. I know how to be kind, I know how to get married, and I know how to spit on the shattered pieces of myself, the better to glue them up again. I think.

By the way, I've got the most terrific profound remark worked out for some underground newspaper when they get around to electing me Slum Goddess of the Week. They'll be asking about my struggle, and I'll say, "My soul has holes in it," and they'll think I'm talking about my shoes, and they'll look down. "Oh, no," I'll say very gently. "It was a birth injury."

One last precaution to ensure my place in history. I've written a review, a review I'll make available to the wire services should they be interested. It's highly adaptable, since it contains many multiple choices.

It reads:

Last evening, summoned to the world premiere of _____'s play (with music) (without music), I became part of an extraordinary, nay, an overwhelming theatrical experience.

The production at the _____ Playhouse is stunning. No expense has been too great, no whimsy too improbable for (author) (director) (author-director) _____ to approve. (He) (She) (They) have given us a complete (sand beach) (slum street) (castle on the Rhine) onstage, along with an (eight) (eighteen) -piece orchestra and half a dozen bathing beauties.

The beauties (so identified in the Playbill) sport a collection of varicose veins I wouldn't have expected to see outside a rest home for elderly waiters. Far prettier is leading man _____, whose muscles are impeccable, but whose diction, mercifully, is not, otherwise we should all have had to listen to much more of (Mr.) (Mrs.) (Miss) _____'s painfully inept dialogue.

The play's theme, (redemption through love) (crop rotation on the veld) (the struggle for peace of mind) (the struggle for plain peace), runs through the script and right out again in pursuit of the actors. But perhaps "run" isn't the word for this faltering display, as the hero trails after a (nightclub singer) (prostitute) (blind flower-seller) (rich person), played by _____. Again, "played" is too strong a word. What _____ does is sing, and that interminably. She is always at least three notes lower than and several beats behind the band, which smiles valiantly throughout. Or maybe they're really just a step away from laughing out loud.

One ray of light does force its brilliance through the more than two hours of otherwise unadulterated murk. An enchanting (child) (woman) (old lady) named Irene Kane, who could give acting lessons to all those better-knowns swarming about her, works ceaselessly in a lost cause.

She is adorable. She has talent, charm, humor and faith. She says those awful lines as though she believes them, and sometimes she even makes you believe them too. She is half waif, half siren, altogether remarkable, as she goes about the business of _____. Someone should rescue Miss Kane from the morass, and the posse forms right here, behind this critic.

I think that ought to take care of everything.

6

Further Correspondence from the Underground—and I Don't Mean Subway

Dear Mrs. O,

Hope you and the babies are well, and your marriage to Lennie (you remember Lennie, your husband?) continues serene. If it should *not* continue serene, please don't tell me about it, because I am up to my lower lip in messes between men and women, and it's all your fault.

Remember when we were discussing how actors are out of work more than they're in work, and how I was going to find me a supplementary income, or quit running up Bloomingdale's bills, cold turkey? We talked of what a fine play reader I'd be, due to my reading excessively fast and forgetting what I've read even faster. I could earn my dollar a day and never be burdened by hangover, since I have such an open mind everything falls right through it.

Well, along those lines, I approached a few people and got a nibble. Do you remember Charlie Lindstron, who runs that true-confession-style magazine? He said I could weed out letters for an advice column conducted by an old lady. Old lady would then, with such legal and medical aid as she deemed necessary, answer the mail I passed along, but she would be spared the initial bother of having to decipher scrawls from unfortunates, maniacs and creeps.

The advice column appears every month (accompanied by a box that implores, "Let Me Help You") in this fifty-cent periodical which details recherché sex practices of illiterates for illiterates. (It details them, of course, illiterately.)

The first few days' reading shook me up. Everybody's troubles seemed so terrible, and I cried and felt guilty about deciding which poor souls should get help. First batch I took back to Charlie, I handed him the answerable dozen, and pointed to a sackful of rejects I was returning. "What happens to them?"

"Nothing," he said.

"But that's so heartless," I said.

He glared at me. "What do they want for fifty cents?"

The other day I found out something Charlie doesn't know. A kind soul in his office has had a form letter printed (it advises faith in God and having self-respect) and she sends it off to every correspondent not personally answered by the old lady. Offhand, I'd say the receivers of the form letter come out ahead, because if the old lady chooses to answer your letter in print, by the time her advice appears in the magazine it's at least four months since you've solicited her help. For a guy who's, say, dodging the police by hiding out under his front porch, the soft spring rains have turned to winter snows, and a warm cell's beginning to look good to him.

After a while the letters sort themselves into distinct types. A big load comes from romantic teen-agers. "I love him more than life itself, and I would go all the way with him," is the gist of these. Sometimes she loves him more than life itself but she won't go all the way with him because he'd lose respect for her. Sometimes she's gone all the way with him and is pregnant and

45

regrets having gone all the way with him, but by the time the old lady answers this kind of problem, the baby's been born, christened or given up for adoption, as the case may be, and any answer at all is academic.

Maybe the sufferer's writing down of his suffering is therapeutic. I hope so.

For me, the worst thing is trying to decide which letters the old lady will enjoy answering. Is she anxious to deal with the sixteen-year-old who wants to "stop people from saying that I'm a whore which I'm not and have know intentions of becoming one"? Or the teen-ager who writes, "Him & me has been through the hell & heaven of love"? Or the lady who feels, "after laying the field," that marriage is dull? Or the kid who states somberly, "I have been going steady with Oliver McMuffin for 25 days, and in that time, I have had one (1) date!"?

What about the lady whose husband keeps "running at a 19-year-old girl. Tell me what to do if he keep running at that girl." And the lady whose husband wants her to "stupe below normal sex." To say nothing of the lady who has yeast. "I have yeast," she says. "My doctor doesn't know, and if you ask me, he doesn't care." There's a girl so "bole legged" she doubts if she will ever get a date, and another who questions the efficacy of prayer. "I'm ashamed I don't believe in God no more, I never pray, and I don't care about him," she says, adding that now she's stopped praying, "I've got luck, and troubles seem lighter." Every time she slips back into prayer, disaster follows. "I prayed a few weeks ago, and my father broke his toe, my sister was hit by a car, I lost my purse (I had about $35 in it, and also other things)," she catalogues mournfully.

One of the most unanswerable letters was in this month's batch, but it was also one of the most fascinating. It came from an eighteen-year-old named Bessie Jo Elinor Ordway, who said, "My boyfriend, he are 22, and his name are Lemuel Blagden. We decide to marry and some bitch of Florida arrive. He want her to leave and she won't. Her name are Rapunzel S. Garland. She have try to root work me and him. She drinks, she's no good, she is married, but she kill her husband. Help me. Bessie Jo Elinor Ordway." A P.S. from Lemuel Blagden ran, "Help us. I don't like this girl, her name is Rapunzel Garland. How about making her leave me."

Across the bottom of the letter ran the legend, "Help us." Underneath this it said:

> My name is Bessie Jo Elinor Ordway.
> My boyfriend name is Lemuel Blagden.
> Not her.
> Her name is Rapunzel S. Garland.

Don't you wonder what root work is, and if Rapunzel did kill her husband (in which case she isn't really married anymore, technically speaking), and who will win Lemuel?

Voodoo victims are arriving not single spies, but in battalions. I've got a testimonial from a woman who insists she's being bewitched, but only when she crosses the state line into New Mexico. "Every time we come to New Mexico, my whole life seems to go wrong, my marriage, and even me. It seems we have a lot of quarrels. I lost inrest in him. Every day I keep losing inrest in him and hate him too. I'm not imagine things either. I would be very graceful if you would write me as soon as possible."

In front of me now is a letter from a lady who's taking issue with another lady whose letter was printed last month. "I agree that her husband is getting his sex satisfaction elsewhere; I disagree that she talk's about it to lady friends. What they don't

47

no don't hurt them. My husband is the same so this wife (me) got her sex affairs right in her own home by a student and a foreign student he's a Ceylon. No one knows and this was free no charge. And she was very much satisfied."

I would be very graceful if I could figure out a way to lose this work. If you don't come up with another idea for a means by which I can earn petty cash, I am going to write a letter to the old lady and sign your name. I am going to say you are having a fling with a Ceylon and your husband doesn't know anything about it, and you are feeding your children acid so they will freak out in the Peter Cooper playground and not interfere with your trysts. Then I will see to it that the old lady's answer gets sent to Lennie's office, and you'll be sorry.

Your adoring sister,

C

7

"A Odd, Odd Person" and Other Role Models

Strasberg told us students that one trouble with actors (after they get successful) is they'd rather sit around Sardi's with other actors than fraternize with human beings. Thus they spend their lives almost totally out of communication with what should be the wellsprings of their art. He didn't say it so pompously. What he said was if you sat around Sardi's with actors all the time, you tended to forget how real people looked or talked or behaved, and since most plays were about people, not actors, this was a shame.

Lee being my idol, I resolved never to let myself be seduced by this danger. Wherever I went, I pledged, I would soak up the various facets of human behavior, the myriad sounds of human speech, as a thirsty plant spring rain. I would avoid actors, reach out towards mothers, pushcart peddlers, beggarmen, thieves, find folk poetry among the folk.

The trouble was, I didn't go anywhere.

And on the rare occasions when I left home, I took a taxi. Both ways. Now, in my opinion, a study of *homo sapiens* which is confined to cab drivers will run you just as crazy as though you were concentrating on actors. So I broadened my scope to include cleaning ladies.

I knew many cleaning ladies. When I wasn't venturing forth

in cabs, I was home watching the different cleaning ladies clean. Or charging around trying to clean up before the cleaning ladies got there, so none of them would decide I was unfit for her cleaning. I knew a char who kept her customers terrorized at mop point. "I quit him," she would say of one who hadn't lived up to her standards. "I would no sooner finish in my bathroom than one of his messy friends would want to go in there and use it, so I just quit him."

You had to eat all your meals before nine o'clock in the morning on the day that lady came, because she wouldn't let you into the kitchen either. "You just keep out of my nice clean kitchen," was the tentative way she put it.

Obviously, you can't have a heart-to-heart with anybody who won't let you in the same room with her, so my research flagged during the days of that woman's tenure, but I can't blame it all on her. I'm a bit phobic myself. I grew up scared of dogs, rabbits, flies, ants, feathers, snails, worms, tripe, tomato soup (I knew it was burning my throat and giving me tonsil stubs), the dark, the light, and people. I was the kind of kid who didn't like to admit she'd lost her faith for fear of hurting God's feelings. So it was hard for me to hold seminars on life and death when I couldn't get my mouth open. But if I left much to be desired as a conversationalist, as an eavesdropper I was peerless. (A date once told me if he ever took me to dinner again he was going to sit at the next table, where he would get all my attention.)

How can you eavesdrop on a cleaning lady, though? You can't hear them over the vacuum cleaner.

Given my extreme diffidence (the other side of egomania, my husband tells me gravely) and my propensity for secret listening, I wasn't getting anywhere with the research, until I resorted to belles-lettres. Writing broke the ice. I learned about brevity from the very first cleaning lady with whom I corresponded.

She was a West Indian of few words—all of them unintelligible—but when she took pencil in hand she achieved splendor. The following memo is all I have left of her. "Dear Kane," it said. "I have broke hair dryer. Will pay half. Truly yours, House Maid."

Truly mine, House Maid, was succeeded by a Scotch dumpling who turned the rooftop paradise in which I was then dwelling (a corrugated tin room, stuck into deep tar, set off by an elegant red-and-gold front door bearing the legend MOUNT VERMIN) into a bide-a-wee home for injured pigeons. Pigeons is another thing I grew up scared of, pigeons sick or well, but this Scots Florence Nightingown (as Amos and Andy used to call a do-gooder) kept hauling pigeons off window ledges and crooning "Puir wee lom" into their dirty, mean, rabid ears. Or what passes for ears on pigeons.

Florence gave way to an Irish philosopher, and her I understood.

I was used to Irish girls, since my mother had always got them straight off the boat, before they'd learned to ask for American money. This meant she didn't come up with too many kids who'd worked in Windsor Castle, so there was incessant warring between her and the slavey of the moment. New girl would arrive, start to serve dinner, appear in the dining room doorway with, say, a cooking pot full of boiled potatoes. Mother would look up, horrified, and say icily, "Go put those potatoes in a bowl, Mary Margaret." Two minutes later, new girl would reappear still bearing the pot of potatoes, but the pot would now be nestling in a bowl.

To give my mother her due, during our impoverished periods, when we didn't have help, she treated me exactly as she had the other servants. I would creep away from the dinner dishes toward the living room, hoping to overhear grownups talking about sex and murder and high prices, but all I would overhear was "Get back in the kitchen, Scullery."

(I have a friend who tried to hurl himself into the middle of a political discussion when he was a little kid. That didn't work either. "You just Roosevelt-stinks yourself right up to bed, young man," was all *he* got for his pains.)

The Irish philosopher was an artist.

Describing a miserable mood she couldn't shake, she'd say, "I was goin' around with that awful deep sighin' down inside." Describing an inferior barbering job inflicted on a neighbor, she'd say, "Her hair looked turrible; it looked like the cat eat it."

She couldn't understand how a family with $150 a week could be unhappy. "If my husband made $150 a week, I'd go sit in the park every day, I'd go to the movies."

It's got to be one of the hardest dollars to come by, the dollar earned by getting down on aging knees to scrub up other people's messes, but humor leaped out of Mary's shoe-button eyes, and when she retired, the friend she sent to take her place was equally valiant. The friend, also a Mary, had a husband who drank and cheated on her and stole her money, and she suffered rackingly from what she called "the broonik-al." Philosophers like David Susskind are always trying to figure out why so many "poor" people listen to soap operas. It's because their lives are like that.

Mary II was followed by the African Princess, who brought along Chester Hagen to do the heavy work. And it was Chester who told the strange tale of a woman for whom he occasionally cooked dinner.

"She is a odd person," he said. "A odd, odd person. She's one of them New Orleans Creole people. Very odd. Take her blood one day, it'll be type A, next day it'll be type B."

Then he went off, to cook and take blood, most likely, but I never forgot him.

The African Princess forgot him instantly. She had a low opinion of human nature, this opinion having been engendered by rudeness piled on rudeness which she'd suffered at the hands of everybody in the world, including babies in their carriages.

Once, she said, she'd forgotten herself long enough to coo at such an infant. "Oh, what a cute little baby," she'd observed, in response to which the apparently sleeping baby had perked right up, opened its eyes and answered, "Ah, shut your mouth."

La. Metra Pole was the other name the African Princess went by, and she insisted that you spell it with a period after the La. "L-a-period, Metra Pole," she would say, standing over me as I wrote out her checks.

I learned about the blood royal coursing through her veins (whether type A or type B, I couldn't say) because she was furious with another of her clients. The other client was an actress, married to a sports car enthusiast (he was really a gold smuggler, but she couldn't introduce him that way at parties), and she had a governess for her children. This governess, the actress had told La. Metra, was a countess who'd fallen on evil times, and who had to be treated with the respect due her exalted rank.

La. Metra, repeating this story, quivered with indignation. She pulled herself up to her full four and a half feet, and spoke in trembling tones. "How does *she* know that *I* am not an African princess? There is plenty of princesses in Africa, and we are all related!"

Mostly what stirred La. Metra to animation was any kind of disaster. Suggest to her a lunch of shrimp salad, and she would decline with thanks. "I don't eat that. I went on a picnic once and I watched my cousin eat some shrimps and in one hour she was dead."

The death toll in La. Metra's family had been heavy, the deaths instantaneous and often caused by locked bowels. "I had a twin, died at seventeen years," La. Metra would say mournfully. "Locked bowels." The listener would start to commiserate, but La. Metra wasn't done. "My daughter had a twin died at seventeen months. Locked bowels."

It starts you worrying, I can tell you. How do those bowels lock, and is there any warning? Or are you just standing there singing "K-K-K-Katy," when you're felled like an ox?

Some of La. Metra's relations had gone in other ways. "I lost a brother burned up in a fire," she confided. "He was only two years old."

This grim snuffing out of a baby brother had left La. Metra with a nose for trouble. Once she'd warned a neighbor that she smelled smoke, and the neighbor had ignored the warning, whereupon "this woman was burnt complete out," La. Metra reported with, I'm sorry to say, a certain satisfaction.

To appease the gods of flame, La. Metra said a little prayer every time she left her apartment, if only to go to the supermarket. "Bless this home from theff and fire," she would intone. It worked fine.

There had been other tragedies in the Pole family. La. Metra's brother's wife—her brother's *late* wife—had been driving across the bridge up near the Polo Grounds, and "she lost control of her car, and broke her neck."

La. Metra's brother had taken this very badly. "He cried for a good six months."

It got so I worried La. Metra was going to run out of family —her only surviving auntie was old, and not a bit well—but when that happened she simply switched to the woes of her friends. "How is Mrs. Soandso?" I would ask, and La. Metra would shake her head. "Not so good. I took her to the doctor. He said some type of a pus was on her vein, and the blood would rush down and settle in her instep."

The only person I ever heard tell of who could compete with La. Metra, anguish for anguish, was a hillbilly songwriter and roper (he referred to himself as a co-song writer) who sent a publishing company a tract about himself because he was looking for some publicity.

His life was a saga of disaster, but he hadn't noticed it. He told a Gothic tale—in the third person—so simply, so sweetly, it brought tears to the eyes. In grammar school, he'd "hated music and failed in every subject." He'd been trained as a barber, "but disliked it." He'd married his childhood sweetheart, who'd divorced him eighteen years later. This had left him "shy about girls." He didn't drink, gamble or smoke, and he could "sing some, but because of a throat ailment he quit." All those close to him had gone to their rewards, and he'd had to stop playing the piano "because of his fingers."

I don't like to think about what happened to his fingers. I don't believe I'd really want to know.

8

Joo-id-ism Takes a Ride

I met a man who bridged the gap between housework and taxi driving when our paths crossed in Nassau. He was driving a cab, but previously, so he said, he had been butler to the Duke and Duchess of Windsor. He was full of misinformation, and it was a pleasure to listen to him ramble on. "That house owned by movie actor Brenda Frazier," he would say. In his mouth, Huntington Hartford became Henneken Hartford, and the late Sir Harry Oakes, the late Sir Harry Oats. Passing a cemetery, he waved one hand airily. "Those graves are not permitted to open."

Thanking heaven for small favors, I came back to New York.

The New York cab driver doesn't need me to put in my two cents' worth about him—he's been immortalized by experts—but the proper study of mankind is man, and an actor needs grist for his mill, and taxi drivers are meat and grist to me. I worship them.

The first driver whose words I ever committed to memory was looking for a rich woman. "But every girl I meet just tore her last pair of stockings, or she hasn't had a meal in a week."

My father said that cab driver and I were soul mates, since I was drawn to losers. (My father once met a fellow who owned a yacht, and he showed this fellow a picture of me, and the boy said, I like her, I love her, what's her phone number, we'll get married, or words to that effect—you can't believe everything my father says—and my father claims he told the boy to forget it. "She won't go out with anyone unless he needs an overcoat.")

New York cabbies don't like to admit they're working for you; they like to imagine you're on the streets to convenience them. If you're going across town, instead of to Kennedy, they take it as a personal affront. I've been berated by a driver complaining that he hadn't had a single fare to the airport all day. Not one. "Ha ha," he cackled. "It ain't worth it." I didn't know what wasn't worth it, but I stayed still. "You just wait," he said. "When I'm ready to go home, some joker'll get in my cab and say Kennedy. I'll pull him right out. 'Take a walk, Charlie,' I'll say."

I have encountered a driver who yearned for the good old days of the Depression—"Janes used to t'row themselves at you, you could shack up for doughnuts"—and a driver who had bad luck in amateur contests. "I was on some amateur hours playing guitar, but I never could win because just before me they put on several ballet dancers, and I'd had it."

There was the driver who'd admired *Greenwillow,* one of Frank Loesser's few flops—"The scenery come on and off beautiful. Without interruption"—and the driver who'd come into big money when he was least expecting it. "It was very nice. All I had to do was follow along behind this funeral until they got to Newark. It's far-er to Kennedy than to Newark, but the fare to Kennedy is only four-sixty, and the fare to Newark is fourteen dollars."

Certain drivers will confide their innermost joys and griefs to strangers, the driver-passenger relationship resembling that between a psychoanalyst and his patient. The driver, or patient, talks into empty air; the passenger, or analyst, sits behind him, unseen and murmuring discreet "Hmm"s from time to time.

In a way, a passenger is better than an analyst, because doctors have been known to doze off, whereas the ferocity of New York City traffic keeps a rider on the qui vive at all times.

(I know an actor whose analyst fell asleep twice, both times while the poor actor was chewing over harrowing details of his *affaires de coeur*. It made him feel he must be an extremely boring lover, and very nearly turned him against women. In a moment of misplaced brotherliness, the actor entrusted my husband with this painful information, and my husband was overjoyed. After that he used to phone the actor very late at night. "I can't sleep," he would say. "Would you mind telling me about your sex life?")

Drivers will sometimes warn you against a life of excesses— "All I lived for was drinking, gambling, making love, and I woke up thirty-five, and I said, 'Where has it gone?' "—but more often their thoughts turn happily to wicked women, the most wicked of whom they believe to be actresses.

They disclaim this belief if they think they've hurt an actress's feelings. A driver told me he had a friend, a metal finisher, who, after coming in first in some contest, had won a date with an actress. "But I don't mean no whore or anything," the driver said.

Many drivers have themselves been in show business, and will name-drop you to a fare-thee-well. I rode with a chap who bragged he'd known all the movie stars under their real names, and then proceeded to demonstrate. "What do you think the late Robert Taylor's real name was?" I knew what Robert Taylor's real name was, because I'm an old movie magazine collector. His real name was Spangler Arlington Brough. But I didn't want to spoil the guy's fun. "What?" I said. "Arlington Spanger," he flashed back, quick as a wink.

And there was the driver who'd once had a contract with William Fox. "Jersey was the mecca then. The studios were in

Jersey. I went out to Hollywood at seventy-five dollars a week, in the days when men with families were only making twelve. I finally got bored. I was in a show in Boston, and I didn't have any kind of part, so I quit. I went into the jewelry business, diamonds, rubies, etc. They all know me on Forty-seventh Street. I could go to work for them, but I'm proud. Pride, what is that? Have I still got any? I guess so. So I work the cab, but I'm putting some money away, and I'm going back in the jewelry business."

What wanderlust had lured him out of the jewelry business before, he never said.

My all-time favorite cabby was a man (Jewish) with a son (Jewish) and a daughter-in-law (Catholic). Religion was his preoccupation. He'd pondered the histories of movie stars (from Elizabeth Taylor to Sammy Davis, Jr.) who'd embraced his faith but hadn't fooled him. "You think Elizabeth Taylor knows anything about Joo-id-ism?" he cried. "If Elizabeth Taylor understands Joo-id-ism, I will give you a free ride to Darien, Connecticut."

What was really nagging at him was his daughter-in-law's perfidy. She had promised to be a Jewish wife and now, instead, she was trying to make his son be a Catholic husband. "And that boy done everything for her," the driver said. "Why, when she was pregnant, he bought her a crib, he bought her a maternity dress. . . ."

My son the sport. The lecture ended with a summary of Catholic Church interdicts (observed by his daughter-in-law) against various books and movies. The list being comprehensive, he was still at it when we'd reached my destination.

I paid him and left, but his voice followed me down the street. I looked back. He was leaning his head out of the window. "And *Last Tango*," he bellowed, "by no means can she see!"

59

I don't know. I did just what my teacher said, went out and studied human nature, and now I've got a headache, and I feel this urge to ruin myself. First, a quick sneak over to Sardi's, and a nip or two with the Lunts, then to find a place where *Last Tango* is showing, and go whole hog.

9

It Is Better to Be a Rich Person's Dog than a Whole Poor Person

When Strasberg advised us to study real people, he didn't say anything about confining ourselves to the working classes. (Some seasons they revive Odets, some seasons it's Noel Coward. You've got to be able to swing both ways.)

I thought it would be simple to soak up the rich and their essences, because I'd been reading Stanislavski. "An aristocrat always carries a top hat, wears gloves and a monocle, his speech is affected, he likes to play with his watch chain or the ribbon of his monocle," Stanislavski wrote.

I hopped out, gathered the equipment called for—hat, gloves, monocle, watch chain, ribbon—hopped back in again and waited for a call to play a czarina.

While waiting, I read Stanislavski's next line and got a rude surprise. "These are all generalized clichés supposed to portray characters," said the master.

Aha. There was more to it. I was going to have to creep about studying the rich the same way I'd studied the workers, in order to be able to "create individual personalities."

But you can't study the rich in Stuyvesant Town; the rich don't hang out there. In Stuyvesant Town you've got your common schoolteachers and your straight bicycle thieves.

So right after a schoolteacher scolded me for talking in the elevator and a kid stripped my bicycle in the carriage room, I moved.

I took a place with a terrace, as befitted my new station. (My new station was Twenty-third Street.)

A terrace is a must if you want to wallow in the psyche of a rich person. Before you put your behind in a butter tub (something my grandma always devoutly wished for me) you must put your behind on a terrace. One of the reasons the rich get robbed so often is because they have terraces. Another reason is because they are rich. But enough of generalizations about terraces. Specifics are what makes an actor great.

Specifically, on some afternoon—I forget the exact date—I was lounging on my terrace, considering the high blind wall of a factory which kept any harmful rays of daylight off my body, and sighing over the beauty of it all. The very chair on which I lolled was a gift from God (it had blown onto my premises one windy night, and the people above me disclaimed any knowledge of it, which I couldn't understand, since while it was rusty and kind of lurched to one side, it was better than what I had, namely nothing).

I was looking over at the red-and-white sign which spells out SHAFTWAY, and the guy upstairs was running around in full view in his drawers, and the exhaust fumes from a nearby air conditioner were wafting over me, and I cried, "I wonder what the poor people are doing!"

Already I was beginning to think—and to behave—like a pampered darling. No more spitting, or wiping my mouth on the tail of my sheepskin coat. (These are two ways Stanislavski says will stamp you for a peasant, superficial though such stamping is.)

But what should my next step be? Brushing up on languages, I decided. (The American rich have to know many languages because, in a democracy, we hire servants without regard to race, color or creed.)

My Spanish is limited to *Hoy Dos Peliculas,* which I picked up off a movie marquee on Fourteenth Street. Still, I believe it is my sacred obligation to make some effort to *habla,* particularly since I am very big with Latins.

A Spanish lady once wrote me a fan letter in English. "Why do I like you so much?" she inquired, and then she answered herself. "I simple do not know."

I simple know and I will simple tell her.

It's because *I do my homework.* That woman was undoubtedly a millionaire or a king or a notable writing under an assumed name. The fantastic thing I've discovered since I turned my attentions from the poor and obscure to the showier classes is that *I am catnip* to the famous! They cannot get their fill! Whenever I come too close to a famous person, he or she goes ape.

I credit Stanislavski almost entirely, and because I am not vain I will cite a mere spoonful of the compliments poured over me by the bucket as quick as I appear in the company of luminaries and they get to marveling at the wonders of me.

Joan Bennett, on the acuity of my vision: "I don't see how you can work with all that hair in your eyes."

George Abbott, on the softness of my voice: "Sing louder."

Josh Logan, on the breadth of my talent (after a dramatic audition): "Have you ever thought of comedy?"

Greta Garbo and I have achieved perfect understanding, because she respects my need for privacy. When we pass one another on the street, I don't bother her and she doesn't bother me.

Queen Elizabeth the II, on the other hand, has gone too far to show her admiration. I read that she actually contracted gastroenteritis and had to spend a day in bed, probably because she'd found out there was a history of that miserable ailment in my background. (The first time I got gastroenteritis, my grandmother called the doctor, who came, saw, said, "Gastroenteritis," and departed. Later I heard my grandmother on the phone discussing the case. "She's got gas and arthritis," my grandmother said.)

Queen Elizabeth really troubles me. She could have chosen another way to show me how she felt. I don't require any such demonstration of solidarity. But that's the problem. Where I'm concerned, the famous lose all discretion.

The straight (nonfamous, infamous) rich are crazy about me too.

Or they would be, if they knew me. Because, thanks to Stanislavski, I don't consider myself too good to study them. There is no rich person so far gone you can't learn something from him. For instance, when Miss Minnie Cushing got married, she told *The New York Times* she didn't have any special champagne at her wedding. "Just the same old Heidsieck, or whatever," she said.

Well, I'd always thought the rich sashayed around saying, "It's an amusing little white wine. We call it Energine." Which proves you can't depend on old Warner Brothers movies for a proper education, especially when you're planning a life in art.

Like Miss Minnie hinted, the old ways are the best.

Since I started studying the rich, I've changed. Now, when I'm preparing for a gig as an heiress or a debutante, I will not share a dinner table with a chef and/or his wife. If, by inadvertence, I discover a chef and/or his wife at my table, I have them removed. This is a trick I learned from Robert D. L. Gardiner of Gardiner's Island, whose ways are so old he's the only person (outside of me, his pupil) who remembers them.

64

Picture the scene. The great Henri Soulé has died. His great Pavillon restaurant is reopening under the direction of the great Claude Philippe, with a great gala benefit dinner, to which Mr. and Mrs. Robert D. L. Gardiner, of Gardiner's Island, have been invited.

The Gardiners come but, according to *The New York Times* again, rise "shortly after they were seated at a banquette in the bar. Mr. Gardiner claimed their coats and prepared to leave. He waxed indignant about the seating plan. 'They obviously don't know too much about New York society. I'm the 16th Lord of the Manor, and I don't intend to sit with a chef and his wife,' he said, referring to the other couple at the table to which he had been assigned."

The other couple "was hastily removed."

Whether the other couple was put to death, or served in the kitchen, I don't know, but I do know if you read the *Times* (it baffles me how Stanislavski made do without it) and use your horse sense (we're dealing, don't forget, with the horsy set here), you can pick up these tips which will render you indistinguishable from the gentry.

At that same Pavillon party, Mrs. John Barry Ryan III taught me something else. Poring over the details of how *she* behaved, I formulated a rule: Don't go to dinner somewheres and cavil if there's no caviar. Don't say, "I was led to believe there would be caviars of all colors at such an upper-crust feed." Make do, as Mrs. III does, with the *foie gras*.

"Of course I love caviar," Mrs. III said gracefully, "but Philippe is terribly excited about the *foie*. He found it himself."

I have been inspired by this to create a parlor game. It's called Find the *Foie*, and the winner gets a goose. *Honi soit qui mal y pense.*

I would advise all actors who wish to play royalty to keep their eyes open. The Gardiners didn't throw that fit yesterday, and I believe Miss Minnie is already divorced from the "old Heidsieck" chap, and the great Pavillon has closed for good, but the lessons left behind are fresh as the day they were printed.

And once you've discovered how to comport yourself in the best places, and can transfer this gift to the boards, you must not stop there. Suppose you are called upon to work with a dog of undistinguished lineage. Can you bring such a mutt up to snuff in the rehearsal time allotted you? Can you train him so that he can pass for the dog of a gentleperson? Once more the *Times* is helpful. Back in 1969, they printed a story about a gray poodle named Joie de Vivre who owned a beige mink coat with horizontal sable stripes and who lunched every day with his mistress, Mrs. F. Raymond Johnson, widow of "a merchandising executive," at Pavillon.

The story explained how Joie liked to eat caviar from a spoon and drink champagne from a glass, and pointed out that his mink was exactly like Mrs. Johnson's. (He and she also had baby-leopard coats.)

Whenever Mrs. Johnson went out to lunch, Joie just settled down in the cloakroom and took his nourishment. "Two medium-rare lamb chops, served on a silver platter with a side order of carrots," said the *Times.*

As far as I know, Mrs. Johnson ate at a regular table.

(At home on Fifth Avenue, Joie breakfasted—off his own tray —in bed with his mistress. "He has Special K with fresh strawberries and some coffee—just like I do," Mrs. Johnson said.)

Moral: It is better to be a rich person's dog than a whole poor person.

(I know this is true because I once saw a poor person. She was trying to buy salmon in a delicatessen, and she said, "It should have a broad back," and the clerk shook his knife at her.

"Lady," he cried, "you wanna eat it or you wanna put a saddle on it?" Henri Soulé would *not* have behaved like that.)

When I decided to polish up my aristocratic tendencies, in order to be hired by theatrical offices specializing in plays about wine-tasting, sexual orgies and other preoccupations of the rich, I also resolved to look more substantial. I realized a raincoat, and sneakers with a piece cut off from the time I broke my right big toe, just wouldn't inspire confidence in the play producers of this brainwashed city where money is king. Money makes the mare go, they used to say. (And it certainly made Jimmy Walker and Mayor O'Dwyer step lively.) I was going to take as my model Joie, who was acceptable anywhere because his wardrobe included white tie and tails and a cowboy suit. Until I found, in *Town and Country* magazine (the *Times* is not the only source of tips for climbers), a picture of a couple reported to be "always on the go. Mostly in pursuit of the sun circuits, summering on Long Island, where main magnets are tennis, golf and beaching."

And what did they wear in those pursuits? Well may you ask. Both sported "marvelous, double-breasted navy hopsacking blazers, over straight, superbly cut white trousers, flag-colored silk scarves."

And where had they got these spiffy threads? At an East Fifty-seventh Street tailoring establishment where they cut their cloth according to your measure.

I knew I had to get me one of those blazers. I didn't care that it cost $125. I didn't care that it didn't cover the base of my bottom (giving me a look rather more ripe and round than long and sleek); I wanted that piece of hopsacking which would equip me to enact Dina Merrill's mother.

But the Fifty-seventh Street establishment had other plans for me. It seemed they'd recently made a yellow pants suit for a lady about two feet tall. Somehow she'd managed to crawl in there—through the letter slot, I guess—and she'd ordered this outfit, and the tailors, presented with her dimensions on paper, had refused to believe the evidence of their eyes and had sewn up a pair of pants and a coat which were more appropriate to a female of average proportions.

Now, tiny though she was, this lady was a warrior. So she'd refused to accept the costume. Her try-on session must have been exciting. Pants legs lying in folds all around her on the floor, proud little head barely emerging from the coat collar, tiny fists, muffled in yards of sleeves, trying to get out and beat the air, yips of rage resounding through the fitting room.

And shortly after she'd stalked away on her brief, furious limbs, I'd come along, and been offered her pants suit. It was a bargain. Only $250 for the coat, and another fifty clams for the pants. I felt that outfit, made for a lofty—well, perhaps "lofty" isn't quite the proper word for so truncated a goddess—rich lady, was my entry into the world of actors Cecil Beaton wouldn't curl his lip at, and I bought it.

It does have a roll over one shoulder which makes me look the teeniest bit hunchbacked, but if I keep my right arm up in a kind of insouciant salute, it hangs pretty good. And strengthens the muscles in my arm besides.

The idea of going into hock in order to look like the *dernier cri* may be frightening to you less plucky thespians, but you *must* overcome your timidity. *Encore,* you may be helped by my own experience with a newspaper article about the designer James Galanos.

"Nobody could mistake his clothes for $99.95," one customer had told the paper. "His things look expensive, even on the inside."

There I was, on the shady side of twenty-one, and I'd

managed to live all that time without being hit by a car, but I'd never known $99.95 wasn't expensive. When I think how close I came to being irrevocably stamped "working class," I shudder.

I have an actor friend who isn't so luxe as I, and he says you can keep the newspapers *and Town and Country,* that he was scraping bottom, playing nothing but chimney sweeps and dishwashers, until *Esquire* came along. *Esquire* helped him break through the class barrier by running an article that explained how to avoid being flunked by the flunkies in gourmet eating places.

My friend gave the *Esquire* advice a dry run. He had his wife phone a famous restaurant and pretend she was a secretary. She said something like, "This is the Count of Monte Crisco's secretary, and M. le Comte is thinking of taking dinner with you, so we are sending over a messenger to pick up your menu."

Then my friend put on a slouch hat, went and fetched the menu, and later his wife called the maître d' back and said, Okay, M. le Comte is going to take a chance on the joint, but just be sure the peasant stew has plenty of fresh peasant, or whatever.

It worked terrific.

But you don't want to be reading about my pitiful friends when you could be reading about Gloria Guinness. Gloria Guinness is another rich lady (like Miss Minnie and Miz John Barry III) whom an actor can study with good results. For several years (alas, no longer) Gloria wrote a column in *Harper's Bazaar,* and it was there, in her columns, that I began to plumb the psychological depths of the aristocracy (all the yellow pants suits in Christendom can't help you if you get onstage and your blue blood is only skin deep). Yes, it was from Gloria that I found out the perils—to the rich—of air travel in a leather miniskirt

69

which hikes up. So what? you may ask crudely. Put your coat over it. Well, that's just what Gloria Guinness thought. But she couldn't. And do you know why not? Because her coat was "with my maid somewhere in tourist class."

If Gloria Guinness doesn't want to come to terms with the uncharted wilds of tourist class, an actor who's set her sights on drawing room comedy can't afford to either. From now on, my maid can just stay home with that pushy chef who was bugging the Gardiners.

My husband has been reading this over my shoulder and shaking his head. He says Sir Laurence Olivier never went through this kind of training, and that I am sipping from all the wrong spigots, sitting at all the wrong feet, wasting my time being the love object of the beautiful people. He says I am bewitched by names too fragile to drop. He says if I will go up to somebody and start bending that person's ear about my dear friends the Gardiners, that person will think I am palling around with the guy who mows the lawn.

The Pope of Rome, my husband says. There's a name. Or Cassius Clay, whose name is so droppable he dropped it himself.

But lunacy, or moon madness, as Rebecca West has pointed out, is a man's disease. They think big. While "idiocy" comes from a Greek root meaning "private person" and applies to females, lost in their finite worlds.

Unlike my husband, I'm content to lift my eyes no higher than high society. The garden variety illustrious suit my purpose.

But from now on, I'm going to try to profit by their experiences without moving close enough so I upset their equilibrium. I've had enough of their lunatic adulation. Hereafter let them worship me at a distance. What good would it do George

70

Plimpton to meet me? And then to come up against the brutal fact that he can never have me?

Plimpton himself finally faced the truth. He must have realized I could never think of him as anything more than a tutor, and he married somebody else. To be sure, it took him five years (he'd met the girl five years before), during which time he was undoubtedly scheming to find ways of breaking down my reserve. Even on his wedding night he didn't sound entirely resigned. "I dreaded this terrible step," he said. "This is rather an awkward day for me."

Little does George know how lucky he was. I've learned the hard way that when an eminence meets me hand to hand, so to speak, someone gets hurt.

To illustrate, let me tell the scary story of my experience with John Simpson Browne, an editor and an old acquaintance, whose ardor for the *haute monde* is not balanced (as is my own) by a restraint which keeps that *monde* at arm's length, or across the foots, as we call them.

I hadn't seen John Browne for several years, until that night at Lüchow's.

Sauerbraten perfumed the air, violins sawed away at the Vienna Woods, and I was sweeping out (they'd have liked me to wash the dishes as soon as I'd finished the sweeping, but I'm not so dumb as all that), when I heard a voice yelling my name. Yelling one of my many names. "Chris, Chris," this voice was yelling.

It was attached to John Simpson Browne. I approached his table and he rose. He flicked a hand at me and then toward a lady seated at his table. "Chris Chase," he said, "Duchess of Argyll."

"What?" I said.

"Chris Chase," he said again, "Duchess of Argyll."

Just plain "Duchess of Argyll," not "Lulu, Duchess of Argyll," or "Her Ladyship, Hassenfeffer, Duchess of Argyll," or however they do it in those circles where Gloria Guinness and her maid muck about.

It would have made Stanislavski sick.

I fell to one knee but the Duchess, having been improperly presented, did not acknowledge my greeting by so much as a flicker of her diamonds. She stared straight in front of her at a space above the sugar bowl, until I retreated, limping.

She was the only duchess I ever met who could resist me. (She was the only duchess I ever met altogether.) But I blame it on John Simpson Browne and his plebeian ways. He could have ruined my relationship with Queen Elizabeth herself if he'd blurted out, "Chris Chase, Queen of England," like that. As it is, it will take more than John Browne to come between Her Majesty and me.

I bet she's hoping I'll play her in the movies.

10

Sex on the Boards

I have never been cast on a couch.

Nobody has ever twirled his mustaches at me and said I would have to pay with my rosy pink body for the break he was about to give me.

Sometimes I feel bad about it. I must be the only girl who ever worked in a George Abbott show that George Abbott didn't take dancing. I've been very close to George Abbott when he was dancing, but that isn't the same thing. I was sitting in a chair across the table from him and his date was how it came about, and Mr. Abbott was pretty mad anyway, because he'd come for the dancing and there, hogging the dance floor, in a gang of spotlights, were half a dozen singers doing old Rodgers and Hart numbers. Some of them from shows Mr. Abbott had directed.

Tapping his foot impatiently, waiting for the entertainment to be finished, Mr. Abbott listened, and his thoughts went back to Lorenz Hart. "Such beautiful words to come out of that unhappy little man," he said, almost tenderly. Then he pointed to my whiskey glass. "If he'd left that alone, he'd have been here today."

I dropped the glass, and it broke all over Hal Prince (who also never took me dancing), and I cut my rosy pink thumbs trying to brush the pieces off him and into the middle of the table, and worrying about my drinking, and my sex appeal, or lack of it.

But surely, you're saying, somebody in the show business must have found you fair. A little. Once. A stage doorman? A delivery boy from the delicatessen? A house doctor?

Well, Mike Nichols did ask me out. My husband wouldn't let me go, but I was pretty smug and told all my friends about it and it got back to Mike Nichols and he said I had a big mouth.

Then a fifteen-year-old boy at Lawrenceville wrote and said he was going to take his life, which he'd been throwing away on beer anyway, if he discovered I wasn't as darling as my picture, and another man accosted me while I was walking up and down the aisles of the 46th Street Theatre collecting money for the Actors' Fund.

I hadn't wanted to walk up and down the aisles. I'd offered to turn my week's salary over to the management if *they* would walk up and down the aisles, but they wouldn't. And then this guy grabbed my hand and closed it around something that felt like a rock, and I must have looked startled, because he whispered kindly, "It's an M&M candy."

Since Rebecca of Sunnybrook Farm could have shared these experiences, it's no wonder the big boys didn't think I was right for any of the parts when they came to cast *Valley of the Dolls.*

To be sure, I have come very close to an orgy. To a bunch of people who'd *been* to an orgy anyway. Sort of close to that bunch. (Though not as close as I came to George Abbott when he was dancing.)

It was at a New Year's Eve party (to which I'd been given permission to go by CBS. My husband was working for CBS that year, and money was tight, and his department had sent out a memo. The company, said the memo, wouldn't be hosting any holiday celebrations, but employees should "feel free to gather in your own homes"). Everybody was sitting around talking about a guest who was scheduled to appear. She'd just been arrested for making a topless movie in the city streets. "She *likes* to take her top off," the In guests were explaining to the Out guests. "She'll come right in here and take her top off. Wait and see."

My husband started biting his nails and singing "Lady of Spain" and behaving in a generally eccentric manner, and I tried to lift the tone of the evening by talking about great books with a man who said he'd just written one, and a columnist for an East Village newspaper sat on the floor and told admiringly of a doctor who allowed the press to eavesdrop on his patients in group analysis.

Then *she* arrived. With her accompanist. That's what she said he was. She had plans to be a singer, once she'd mastered the knack of keeping her shirt on. But the poor girl had no sooner got in the door than some rotter, preying on her weakness, went to the record player and started *Music to Strip By*, and she was undone, and so were her buttons. Before you could say "I can't bear it," she had. "I *like* to take my tits out," she said fiercely.

Shortly thereafter she left, with her accompanist and the writer for the East Village paper, searching for madder music and stronger sauce. And some of the people left behind at the party told a tragic tale.

Recently, it seemed, Miss Topless had attempted to stage an orgy. After she'd got her satyrs assembled, she'd gone into another room, from which she'd emerged eventually, stark naked. Whereupon all her prospective partners had begun to stare at their shoes and talk about Betty Crocker pie crust mix.

"She's not a good orgy leader," explained one of the New Year's Eve revelers. "She's too high-strung. All the good orgy leaders are on the Coast."

It must be so. There must still be some sex rampant in Hollywood, where they invented it. Mark Rydell, a New York actor (he was on a soap opera for years) who went west and became a successful director, told me agents still wheeled starlets through directors' offices, explaining that the starlets were available for love and kisses in exchange for acting jobs. A roll for a role, as you might say.

"But I can't do it," Mark said disapprovingly. "If I did it, I'd lose the only thing I got goin' for me, my old one-two."

"What's your old one-two?" I made so bold as to inquire.

"My objectivity!" he said.

Often I think of him, manfully pushing girls away, hanging on for dear life to his old one-two.

Actually, theatre people talk about sex a lot, and they fool around a lot, and they get into trouble a lot, but mostly their narcissism protects them from heartbreak, since the impressions they make on one another are literally no more than skin deep.

I knew a Hollywood actor, nice-looking, intelligent, and under contract to 20th Century-Fox, which, because he wasn't making giant strides there, he called 18th Century-Pox. One night, in a garden, under a moon, he proposed to me.

I started to twitch. I liked him. I didn't want to hurt him. I had visions of his going home and slashing his wrists because life without me would be dust and ashes. I fell over my tongue, but decided I had to tell the truth. "You're the greatest person I know," I said, lying. "But when you come into a room, my knees don't tremble. I mean, for me, you have no magnetism."

Stricken, he gazed at me. And he said, "I wonder if that's what's holding me back at Fox."

You couldn't break that actor's heart. He didn't have one.

I would like to write about nights of burning kisses, and savagely bitten lower lips, and lesbians vying for my favors, and how I first tried kief in a tent in Katmandu with a hot-eyed devil whose ways were not as yours and mine.

I would get very rich from writing that, and then they would make a movie out of it, and I would get played by Suzanne Pleshette.

That's the bad part.

The other bad part is my sister. She's convinced all actors experience just such absorbing love lives (my dentist, too, long before the law was changed, would never believe I couldn't recommend an abortionist) and that I'm simply behaving lazily by refusing to tell her the details of such passions as Marcello Mastroianni and I have spent together. ("Though we could not speak one another's language, there was no need of words between us. The touch of his fingers made my blood cry out, *Luigi Barzini, antipasto, Santa Lucia,* and like that.")

So, for my sister's sake, I'm putting down everything I've seen or heard along these lines, and if it's boring don't tell me, tell my sister.

I saw a producer-director who combed his hair like Napoleon necking on a stage with a girl whom he was guiding through a private understudy rehearsal. The theatre was dark, and they didn't know I saw them. The only interesting thing about it was that the girl was *my* understudy, and two weeks later the producer fired me and put the girl in my part.

I saw a little star (who drove a little car and had a little valet) take all his little clothes off his little wrinkled body and go chasing through a lake after a lot of equally stripped-down apprentices. The star was drunk, the night was falling, and so was he, and I didn't hang around long enough to find out if he caught anybody.

I saw a character lady in a summer-stock show embark on an affair with a fifteen-year-old boy and, in the same show—I was playing the tomboy kid sister of the beautiful ingenue—I saw

77

the beautiful ingenue embark on an affair with the tub of muscles which was her leading man. I was shocked to my bourgeois roots because the beautiful ingenue had been married a big three months—to her agent—but as we rode back into town on the train one night, she explained that the marriage wasn't apt to last. "He's too old for me," she said. And it turned out she was right.

In Massachusetts, I fell in love with a set designer because, when the set fell down with an ear-splitting crash, he turned to his assistant and said, "They're playing our song."

In Florida, I fell in love with an actor who was in love with the boy who ran the lights.

In Ohio, I fell in love with an actor whose wife didn't understand him. I didn't understand him either. I didn't understand he had a wife.

In the Poconos, Bill Ball said that if we lived together for the remainder of our tour, we could both travel in his car and save a lot of money splitting gas bills, but I don't think he loved me.

In Georgia, Michael Rennie invited me up to his suite for milk and cookies, but I don't think he loved me any more than Bill Ball did.

Milk and cookies. Rabelaisian is the only word for it.

My two serious emotional involvements were with Sir Laurence ("Larry") Olivier and Oskar Werner, but nothing worked out because neither of them would come to the phone.

And though my experience with the Sodom which is Hollywood has been brief, I *have* observed the Gomorrah of Las Vegas.

The first day I reported to a rehearsal hall in Las Vegas, I overheard an entrepreneur procuring, for two wealthy gentlemen, two willing showgirls. Before telling the girls where to find their benefactors, he introduced them—the girls—to one another.

"Veronica, forty-six," he said, "meet Charlotte, thirty-eight." And he wasn't reciting their ages; he was giving their bust measurements.

Las Vegas is basic.

You get in at four in the morning, say, and it's lit up, everything going, supermarkets, barbershops, casinos, and you tell yourself it would be nice to have breakfast before you go to bed, so you try one of the big hotels. You sit at a table and order pancakes, and at the next table there's a man in a tuxedo waving a glass of bourbon around and explaining to his lady, "The seed of cancer is in the coffee bean." Up on the stand, a trumpeter is blowing a tired blues, and through the window you can see pink light beginning to come up across the desert.

It's not like White Plains.

In Las Vegas, the show I was with fell apart. The heat dried up everybody's brains, along with their sinuses. People who'd come out from New York just seemed to walk amok (it was too hot to run). A dancer, who'd kissed her husband a tearful goodbye at Penn Station, moved into a room with a French waiter known only as Bébé. My best friend got a divorce and then turned right around and strung herself out over a Mexican piano player. He was married and had nine children, and everybody knew it but my friend. Old twinkle-fingers could tickle the ivories socko, but he wasn't a big talker.

Another of our fellow performers, a singer, fell in love with a hypnotist who was appearing in the lounge of the same hotel where we were working, and later she left her husband, and the hypnotist left his wife, and the two got married. And divorced.

She had herself hypnotized before the show every night. She said it did her the world of good.

But even in Las Vegas I was a romantic misfit. I got married there, which is considered deadly square, unless you put a paper cup over the handle of your slot machine to signify you'll be right back.

Reluctant to wed (though I've always been enthusiastic about getting engaged), I was found at noon down at the city hall, on the arm of a tall, redheaded person who'd flown out from New York just to argue. Worse still, he'd borrowed the money for the flight, and now he was figuring I'd feed him.

I was saying I had to get back to do the show, wouldn't he like to see the swimming pool, and all right, I *would* feed him, wasn't he getting hungry for his lunch?

He was saying that in New York one had three days to think about getting married, which was more time than a person of my limited mentality could afford to spend thinking for fear of brain damage, that there was nothing to panic about, he had always been very kind to his dog, Joe ("How much will you take for that dog?" "This dog, sir, is not for sale!"), that his mother thought he was aces up, and that he had a fortune in empty beer bottles which could be redeemed for cash the minute we got back to Big Town.

No girl could have resisted him.

The ceremony was brief, but memorable. It featured a spittoon at our feet and the anguished wails of downhearted frails who didn't want to be called away from their secretarial work to be witnesses.

It was okay with me. I didn't want witnesses. I am a secret person, reclusive by nature, fearful of giving a party lest people come in and throw up on the wing chair. I never tell anybody

80

my right name if I can help it, and when I can't help it, I try at least to spell it wrong.

My husband, on the other hand (he that joined hands with me across the spittoon), is so gregarious he interferes on the street if he sees a woman yelling at her kid. ("Leave that child alone, ma'am," he suggests, and the woman generally counters with a suggestion of her own about where my husband can go, and what my husband can do when he gets there, you creep.)

So while I was dressing to go to the theatre, old Paul Revere was out spreading the news.

I didn't suspect, until I took my bow that night and the band struck up "Here Comes the Bride."

Muttering words better muttered than printed, I rushed off-stage and was grabbed by somebody and shoved through a hall and into a vast ballroom where champagne was flowing, and thirty-five Mexican violinists (and my friend's piano player) were launching into "Fascination."

It was a celebration right up a recluse's alley.

And that's about it. I know it isn't enough. I know what people want to read because I want to read it too.

Among the actors I'm personally acquainted with, only one lived any kind of romantic legend. This lady was being kept by a film magnate during the good old days (which was only proper, the film magnate himself being good and old), and one time they were off at sea on his yacht (she preferred being on land, because when they were on land she could tuck him in bed after dinner and go out dancing), and the steward brought her a breakfast tray, and in her egg cup she found an emerald.

What a way to go wrong.

Ah, but it's no use to put on your yellow vinyl sailing suit and go hang around the docks.

Not if you're a girl George Abbott didn't take dancing.

If you're such a girl, you can forget about emeralds, and Sir Larry, and the rest of it.

A girl like that had better be glad she's got that gangling, redheaded beer-bottle baron.

Sex on the boards might be rough, after all.

11

My Beauty Secrets, or Never Let a Whale Bite Your Leg Off

There are certain differences between me and Mark Twain.

Besides the obvious one of gender, and him being a riverboat pilot.

His cynicism is what I refer to.

"I hate to take advice from some people," he said, "when I see how bad they need it."

I'm nothing like that. I take advice from anyone, and I believe I should be empowered to dole some out too. If you accept the old saw about "Those that can, do; those that can't, teach," you'll also have to accept that my ignorance qualifies me to instruct people in many subjects.

I can't speak Chinese, ride a horse, play golf, shinny up a flagpole, make change or ask a cop a question.

I also can't ski, stand up straight, set my hair, grow an avocado or kiss good. (There have been complaints about the last one.)

So, if I were venal, I would instantly open an academy for the illumination and indoctrination of almost everybody in almost everything, and the money would start rolling in.

But I don't operate that way. If you want advice from me, just come around. I give it free.

I frequently say this to people, yet nobody asks my opinion, not even about my beauty secrets. This bothers me *au fond* (I couldn't teach French; I'm too much of a crackerjack at it) because all us important actresses are lookers. In my profession you got to be lovely, and never mind Sarah Bernhardt was plain —have you seen her in a movie lately?

Anyway, I am as beautiful as the next one. (The next one is my husband, and his face may be prettier, but his expression isn't so sweet.)

I try to collect all the beauty tips I can from *other* beauties —a woman cannot be too delectable, especially when she doesn't kiss good—but much of the counseling you get elsewhere is of no earthly use. (I know I admitted, back in my high-fashion chapter, that I was a poor model, but you don't have to lay an egg in order to spot a rotten tip.)

Why, I remember reading interviews with nineteen supermodels, and those models' recommendations were pitiful.

One girl named Cheryl Tiegs came out for "the clean look," and she had "small, sparkling white teeth, as even as ivory beads."

Well, what good did it do me to know that, when my own look is somewhat lived in and my front teeth are all different colors?

A great huge model named Veruschka was a bust, too, when it came to guidance. "If I am in the mood to look very young," she said, "I put to my freckles some more with a brown pencil."

I wouldn't like to tangle with Veruschka—she's bigger than a boxer, let alone a breadbox—but I put to my freckles some more with a brown pencil on a day when I was looking middling old, and I wound up looking middling old with measles.

There was a model who stuck "single false lashes" in among her own natural feathers. One at a time. I tried it. It was terrific. The only hangup is it took twelve hours. By the time I was ready to go out, my husband was already in bed inquiring about when was I going to turn off the bathroom light?

84

There were other tips in that bunch too. One model used mustache wax, and one model concentrated so hard on applying her makeup that she sometimes fainted in the process.

I see no value to any of this, except the hint about fainting, which is sound, since when you faint you fall down, and falling down brings blood to your head and gives you a glow.

Most of those nineteen supermodels said they used no cosmetics—"just a little eye liner and a blusher"—but this is not a good tip either, what with its being a flat-out lie. Else why do they carry those satchels full of paint around with them and why, if you accidentally slap a model in the face, does a piece of her cheek chip off?

No matter. If you're dubious about making a pleat near your eye with surgical adhesive, you've come to the right place. You think I'm making it up about the pleat, but *Glamour* magazine once recommended it as a way of opening up the outside of your eye.

"With a toothpick, apply a dot of adhesive to the base of the false lash at the outside corner. Now place the toothpick below your own lashes at the outside corner and another toothpick about a hairline above the dot of adhesive, and press together, forming a tiny pleat."

I studied that over about nineteen times, and then I tried it and I thought I got it just right, but when my husband came home he said, "Why have you pasted toothpicks in your eyes?"

Enough. I am going to give the women of America, whether they want them or not, my beauty secrets, at absolutely no cost to themselves. Which is more than Luella Cuming did for me.

The reason I mention Luella Cuming is she is a lady who acted like she was going to tell *me* a lot of secrets, but then it turned out she wanted $14.95 for them.

She came on like she was anxious to learn me—and a few

other hand-picked clients—about "social awareness, poise and gracious living."

How I knew she'd picked me out special was the brochure she sent was addressed to "Occupant, Apartment 3A," and that's where I live.

"Frankly, this course is not for everyone," she wrote, "but for those whose interests and activities indicate they have the potential for further social advancement."

It was exciting that Luella believed in my potential, because I hadn't given her any good reason to do so. Perhaps she had seen me crouching beside the stove in some fashionable East Side kitchen one night, while others were in the living room drinking and laughing it up. I just don't know. But the brochure said she was going to sit down with me and give me "the same individual guidance she gives the top executives, society women, diplomats and other important people who attend her Course in New York."

The brochure said Luella's students gladly paid high fees to acquire graces, among them being "how to act toward your escort, how to get a good table without waiting, how to catch the waiter's eye and how to order food and drink that mark you immediately as a person of superior taste."

I'd seen some top executives and society women ordering food and drink, but I never knew where they learned it until I got the brochure from Ms. Cuming. When I was playing in a soap opera at CBS, I took a great interest in Mr. and Mrs. Paley (an executive and a society woman sans peer), but before the brochure came, I thought they drank in all that good breeding with their mothers' milk.

Ms. Cuming promised I'd never again feel nervous or embarrassed, "even in the plushest places," and that I'd be able "to command the center of interest in any group."

Then she broke her pick with me.

She said she was going to divulge the answers to such tricky social problems as:

1. How to reply to an extremely personal question.

2. The best way to "break the ice" with a new acquaintance.

3. The tactful way to get rid of a guest who overstays his welcome.

What's tricky about *those* problems? What's the matter with time-tested answers like:

1. None of your beeswax?

2. How are they hangin'?

3. Haven't you got a home?

Ms. Cuming also said she would give her pupils insights into the relationships between men and women—"You'll discover what a man looks for and expects in a woman"—and that sounded promising, too, until she clued me in that it had to do with being a person of "refinement and warmth."

I thought about it. And I realized Marlon Brando in his whole life was never attracted to a person of refinement and warmth. He just likes those girls with long dark hair and a flower behind their ear. And I decided the hell with good taste; it's back to beauty for me.

It's true enough that one can't share *all* the mysteries of one's bloom with one's readers, because one has certain attributes that are a direct gift from the Creator.

I mean, how can I tell people a way to get flat feet? You're either born with 'em, or forget it.

I did have something to do with the fact that the caps on my front teeth are all different colors. The secret of this is to go to all different dentists, each of whom will assure you he can match your caps perfectly, but each of whom is lying in your teeth.

What happens is your cap always breaks in a strange city. You will be in Boston's Chinatown, daintily nibbling on a sparerib, when your front tooth disengages itself, and the director of whatever disaster you're traveling with won't let you go home to New York, and you can't go onstage without a front tooth because the rest of the cast will think you're trying to be smart, so it's a nice glass Boston tooth (ivory) in a line of New York's finest porcelains (white) and that's simply the beginning. Add a Hollywood molar (beige) and you get part of the picture. The reason I write is I don't like to talk too much because of having to open my mouth.

Now that I look this over, my caps don't sound like a good secret. Maybe the secret is not to eat spareribs. Or Good Humors. I once broke a cap on a Good Humor. After that I had my caps angled so far forward I keep nibbling on my lower lip, but it isn't the same as having Marlon Brando do it. I bet.

However, before I leave the subject of loveliness, I have a few really urgent words to the wise.

Stay cheerful. Suffering makes lines in the face. Another way of saying this is, Never let a whale bite your leg off. I saw a production of *Moby Dick* in which Rod Steiger played Captain Ahab, and one sailor said to another sailor, "Ever since he lost that leg, he's been kinda moody."

Moodiness will make lines in the face as quick as suffering.

Eat plenty of potatoes. This produces a firm, round, unwrinkled appearance exactly like Elizabeth Taylor's.

Eat plenty of garlic. This guarantees you twelve hours of sleep—alone—every night, and there's nothing like rest to give you shining orbs (poetic), peepers (colloquial) or lamps (slang). A diet of potatoes and garlic leaves you oodles of time for reading *Roget's Thesaurus in Dictionary Form* too.

Never admit you're thirty-one. A couple of years ago, four airlines in this country had policies requiring stewardesses to retire soon after they hit thirty, and when a newspaper asked why, an airline executive declared, "It's the sex thing. Put a dog on an airplane, and twenty businessmen are sore for a month."

One of our representatives in Congress, looking into the whole sorry affair, said the airlines needed "to be educated to the fact that they're not operating flying bunny clubs," and another congressman quoted Benjamin Franklin, who'd said that in middle age, feminine allure and sensitivity were enhanced "as in vintage wine."

Vintage eyewash. Never admit you're thirty-one.

There, I've done my best. Told all I knew, and a few things I've only guessed at.

In the end, the master, Cary Grant, whose own beauty is limitless, may have given us the best steer.

"We should all just smell well," he said, "and enjoy ourselves more."

12

More About Loveliness: As the Twig Is Bent, So the Ankle Breaks

Listen, I fear I didn't tell the entire truth in the last chapter. Not that I won't stand by every pointer I gave; only that getting as round as Elizabeth Taylor is not the *entire* answer to gorgeousness and success in the theatre.

An actress should also be tough, and have good muscle tone.

A tough actress with good muscle tone can conquer the universe. And if she's also got a big bosom, it's only a hop from the universe to the Johnny Carson show.

I had a friend who played in a revival of *Desire Under the Elms* down at the Circle in the Square when Rip Torn, George C. Scott and Colleen Dewhurst were raging through the leads. There was a scene where Rip was supposed to hurl Colleen to the ground. One night he threw her down, and she got up, shook herself off and knocked him flat on his piazza. He rose, somewhat put out, and attempted to press her earthward again. She won that round too. "It was," my friend said admiringly, "like they were in a wrestling match and the winner was the one who got best two falls out of three."

Rip Torn quit the show after that, leaving the field to Colleen. She'd won it fairly; she had muscle tone.

My own muscle tone was achieved through going to a gym run by a guy his intimates (among whom I was not numbered) called Nick. (The only thing Nick ever said to me was "Didn't I tole you not to smoke?" to which I answered, "Yes, sir," though I wasn't smoking and never had smoked.)

I first heard of Nick's place when a friend came over to visit. During a lull in conversation, she went into a corner of the living room and stood on her head. Her legs just sort of floated up and hung there, pointed skyward.

My husband did the following: He fell in love with her, he tried to stand on his own head and tore a ligament, and he asked me, through clenched teeth, why *I* was no good at parties.

So one thing led to another, and I asked my friend Marikay where she'd got those legs.

She said Nick.

She said when she'd first gone to Nick, she'd been fresh back from a pig's tour of Europe (that's "Forget the museums, sweetie, wheel me down to Les Pyramides"), she'd just finished nursing a baby and she'd weighed 150 pounds. On her trial visit to the gym, she'd changed her clothes in the bathroom because she didn't want to be seen in the dressing room in her underwear. "I looked all lumpy, like I was wearing my leotard over all my clothes," she said.

Now she had these elegant legs, full of muscle tone.

I had to go to Nick.

Being a natural coward, I enlisted my sister, a game little dickens, who said she'd be glad to come with me, but I'd have to wait until she bought Gucci shoes and a Pucci dress and a Vuitton tote for carrying her gym gear back and forth. She said Nick was confidant to high-fashion models and famous stars of the theatre, who hung around him sipping champagne as they leaped from sawhorse to sawhorse on their elbows, and she, my sister, didn't want to be caught looking as though she lived in a Metropolitan Life Insurance Company housing project, just because she lived in a Metropolitan Life Insurance Company housing project.

Mrs. Onassis went to Nick, my sister said, along with the entire roster of charge customers at Tiffany. "They lunch at Caravelle right after their lesson," she told me, "and they have runs in their tights, and you will look like an ass if you wear that new black nylon Danskin you bought from the guy that sells seconds on Fourteenth Street."

My sister is like Gimbels department store; she's trading up.

She phoned Nick and made an appointment for a test lesson. For two. The guy at the desk had never given a test lesson for two, but he agreed. We showed at our appointed hour, changed clothes and were escorted into a studio with full-length mirrors and dancers' practice bars around the walls.

Our instructor was a good-natured teen-ager, which put us ahead right away. Marikay had been given ("given" is too strong a word; "flicked" is more like it) her test lesson by a member of the Russian nobility who'd viewed her with loathing. At least that's the way she remembered it. "How much do you weigh?" he'd said, and when she'd told him, his lip had curled. She was so happy to be able to say no when he asked if she smoked that she'd added a little gratuitous good news. "I play the piano." He wasn't impressed. "I couldn't *see* my toes, let alone touch them," Marikay mourned, "and when he told me to get up, I lurched across the floor on my stomach and crawled up his pants leg."

My sister and I couldn't even climb up our guy's pants leg. We couldn't do anything. After we walked into the studio, we'd had it. Except for the measurements. We were very good at the measurements because all we had to do was stand there while he passed a tape measure around our arms, legs, waists, chests, weighed us and made secret marks on a record we never got

92

to see. He had us breathe into a gadget that measured how much breath we had. He said I had none. My fighting heart was all that was keeping me going.

He had us lie on the floor on rubber mats and asked us to bend until we started to crack. Then he pointed to rings suspended from the ceiling on ropes, and suggested that we fly. Heaving, straining, with him lifting our backsides up over our shoulders, we disported ourselves. (I'd been acquainted with the idiom *cul de sac*, but I'd never known what it was to have, literally, one's behind in a sling until I came to Nick's.)

Trapeze followed rings, and was even worse. There was also a thing where you hung, back to the wall, by your arms, and tried to raise your legs, but I don't want to talk about that.

Afterward we signed releases. Before you could take classes at Nick's place, you had to agree that it was your problem. If you lost any arms, legs, toes, fingers, tonsils, sunglasses or bikini pants, Nick wasn't responsible. If you got sick and dizzy and had to be taken to St. Luke's Hospital in an ambulance, Nick wouldn't even cry. Your fitness to embark on a career of death-defying aerial maneuvers was between you and your insurance company; Nick didn't want to know about it.

We signed everything, and begged to be allowed to come into a class the next day.

We were 'buked and scorned. Then we were told to go home, lie in hot tubs, swallow aspirins, and phone when the pains went away.

In the fullness of time the pains did go away, and several days later we took our first class under the jurisdiction of a chap named Ivo. Some pupils called him Ivor, and some pupils called him Igor, but I knew his name was Ivo because I'd asked at the desk. I should have asked *everybody's* name while I was at it. Since there was a girl in that class whose name was Lee, and whom I addressed always as Constance. The reason was Ivo's accent. "First we start with Hahnstahnce," he would say, and this girl would get up. Ultimately it became clear that he was talking about handstands, not Lee, but by then she thought I was feeble-minded.

(Accents seduce me. It is a measure of my tiny mind that I forget the Gettysburg Address, but remember for all time Zsa Zsa Gabor's uttering my favorite line in a science fiction movie. Zsa Zsa was playing a kind of worker bee on a manless planet ruled by a wicked queen. A spaceship from Earth landed and a handsome leading man got off, and he and Zsa Zsa had eyes for each other. But the wicked queen had also spotted Handsome, and sent a handmaiden to fetch him. Whereupon, Zsa Zsa looked the camera right in the eye. "I hay dot kvinn," she sniffed.)

Ivo used to say great things, but they were susceptible of misunderstanding. I mean, how about a line like "Approach your toes over the bar"? Even if you've had those toes all your life, you're not always sure how to approach them. Informally, perhaps. "Would you guys care for a beer?" Or with more respect? "Do you gents prefer to work covered up or bare?"

As for my sister, she almost broke her neck (Nick wouldn't have been responsible), because when she was hanging by her knees from the trapeze, Ivo said, "Re-legs down." He meant "Relax," and he meant her arms, but she thought he'd said "Legs down," and she came plunging over into air, howling as she traveled.

After a while, we got so used to Ivo we didn't hear him. When he said, "Go with your head on my shoe down, directly bending your elbows," it seemed sensible, as did "Slowly bend your both calves down in the same time," or "Engage your knees," or "El-ternate your right leg energetically."

94

Sometimes when you came in and he would be distracted, he would explain why. "I counting pipple here."

Ivo used to shake his head as he watched me, and mutter, "No strengt," or "Don't let your elbows to go wild apart," but I hung in there. And up there. And after a while I became an important actress. Breath-wise, I definitely had some. And backside-wise, though I still couldn't keep my end up, so to speak, there was always Ivo to do it for me.

The fact is, I got so radiant with tone and physical allure, I put many a person in mind of Sophia Loren. Especially when that person was standing in a hole.

13

Stalking the Wild Mouse

It would be fun to be a star, if you could do it anonymously. It's the thought of people's encasing my toenail parings in plastic that makes me wonder if I'm up to the demands of the big time.

You don't think I've had close calls? What about the lady on Eighth Street who told me she liked me better than Princess Grace—wasn't that a near thing? And the dirty little kid who followed me home with a camera—didn't he have immortal longings where I was concerned?

The best way to avoid stardom is to keep moving.

Go on the road or play in stock. Nobody can find you out there.

I have sometimes followed this path, which guarantees oblivion, though it has been hard for me since I am morbidly apprehensive about leaving my apartment. In case I might want to go to the bathroom.

New York's indefatigable attorney general, Louis Lefkowitz, once cornered my husband in the corridors of CBS and divulged to him the secret of success in public life. "My boy," he said, "go to the bathroom every chance you get."

But a bathroom shared with strangers reduces me to gibbering.

One might construe from this that I spend a good deal of time in the bathroom oiling my limbs, making up my fabulous face, singing all the parts in *The Marriage of Figaro*, hiding my marijuana in the toilet tank.

It isn't so. I scarcely use the bathroom, but I want to know it's there. Would Mick Jagger line up in the hall with a towel?

I've told advance men (the fellows who travel ahead and make everything ready for the cast before the cast gets to the next town) that I wanted a private bath and was prepared to pay for one, but they've never believed me. I don't make enough money to convince them I'll spend it so frivolously.

Therefore I arrive, look around the dump where they've booked me, and check out.

It's the first step I take when I get someplace.

The second step is to check into the inn where the main snail is staying, on the theory that all stars require bathrooms, television sets and a pitcher of ice from room service every night. This second step has earned me a reputation for being *(a)* a sycophant, *(b)* a climber, *(c)* a lunatic.

What I am is a worshiper of easy living.

Walking around Boston on an evening just a few months before he died, Bobby Griffith, the stage manager turned producer, told me how much he loved the Boston Ritz. "I let them know what time I'll be in, and they run my bath so it's ready when I get there," he said. "And there's a kitchen on every single floor, so breakfast is really hot when they wheel it in in the morning." He stopped and watched a pigeon scuttling through the dusk. "I was poor for so long, sometimes I still can't believe it."

Bobby was a sweet man, and he had patience.

He waited till he was rich before he hit the Ritz.

I stay there now.

Because what if I only get poorer instead of richer? What if the workers of the world unite, and tell me to pick up my things and get down to the pickle factory? What if my brother inherits the dukedom, the law passing over me, in that ugly way it does, because I'm a girl?

The risks are too great, so it's out of the flophouse for baby, and into the Palais de Versailles.

But it isn't just remembrance of bathrooms past that tortures me on the road. It's everything. I anguish over traveling in planes because I'm always scared (the family that flies together dies together is my conviction) and I'm always late, which means I run up the ramp of the first silver bird I see.

Once, coming home from Detroit, I fell into a seat, gasping, and begged the man beside me to be kind. "Is this the airplane to New York?" I asked.

"If it isn't," the nice man said mildly, "I'll buy you a cup of coffee in Boston."

Which brings me back to the Ritz, and the checking-in-and-out habit. Some actors check out as a matter of principle, even when the bathrooms are okay. You could put them in the Lincoln room at the White House and they'd get huffy about it.

I once saw two actors, so drunk they couldn't stand up, making their way across the hotel lobby on their hands and knees, but they nonetheless managed to creep up to the front desk to voice their indignation. Foreshortened as they were, you could only refer to them as being in a state of low dudgeon.

The road makes strange bedfellows, and stranger dinner companions.

For the duration of their tour, people who would ordinarily have nothing to say to one another band together in a clannish, family way. Casts split up, pair off, friendships and enmities are established, it's very intense, yet once you get back home you never see most of your fellow travelers again.

I traveled for a summer with a wonderful actress named Ruth White. We drove together in her car, and it was fine, except that no matter what time we got into a new city, Ruthie had to find the nearest Catholic church. She couldn't sleep otherwise. So at two-thirty on many a morning, in the streets of West Kibble, we'd be hailing perverts and lushes, entreating them to lead us to a house of worship.

My husband says he always resented being older when he came back from a year on the road. To him the road experience, though instructive—and even enjoyable—seemed to hang there, out of time, no serious living being done, one's future suspended until one came home and picked up the threads again, so it didn't seem fair that the aging process shouldn't have been suspended too.

But performers do get to see the world. Parts of the world. (There used to be a park in Vienna which didn't permit actors or dogs.) Sometimes more of the world than they had in mind.

Myself, I haven't got to Vienna yet, but Detroit, Cincinnati and Binghamton aren't to be sneezed at, are they? And what about Mountainhome, Pa.? Or West Fairmount Park, Philadelphia? Arden, Delaware? Somerset, Mass., just down the road a piece from where Lizzie Borden turned herself into an orphan?

I've lived, friends. I've been to California, played in a big musical tent right across the street from Disneyland, and I went to Disneyland every day and rode the Matterhorn, because what the hell else can you do in Anaheim? I've also been to Palm Beach, which is about the fanciest place they've ever let me into.

Lying beside the swimming pool outside Arthur and Virginia Treacher's $125-a-day suite (supplied gratis by the management for the sheer prestige of having Arthur stay there) while a man in a white coat brought us long, cool drinks, I was bade

99

by Arthur to count my blessings. "Little girl," he said, "to live like this you have to be a millionaire. Or an actor."

The Palm Beach playgoers were fascinating. They came to the theatre hung with small furs and full of booze, and as the play progressed the audience split into two parts. One half gossiped with its friends, while the other half slept off its dinner. Either way, they weren't watching the stage. It was a tribal rite, with the cannibals so jaded they couldn't be bothered to eat what was set before them.

In a Palm Beach doctor's office I met a man who warned me to beware of Jewish people, and in a restaurant I met an actress named Margaret Phillips, who was appearing with Eva Gabor in *Private Lives* and who warned me that I'd need several changes of evening clothes.

"Our cast has been invited everywhere," said Margaret Phillips. "And some of these great old houses actually have pipe organs."

Back at the hotel, I surveyed my wardrobe. Blue jeans and a baseball cap for rehearsals. A bathing suit for bathing. And a pink-and-white cotton *schmata* (that's a word I learned from some Jewish person; I think he was my father) for everything else. I felt the way Mrs. Cornelius Vanderbilt Whitney must have felt after her great jewel robbery in Saratoga. "I'll have to go around in nothing but my pearls and my tiara," she told reporters. "I don't know what I'll do."

I didn't know what I'd do either. *Schmerz* engulfed me. I should be seated below the salt in all the great old houses. I should be made to stand by the very lowest pipe of the organ. I should be sent off to bed without any aspic.

My agony was premature. I wasn't invited anyplace. Not to one old house. Not one single swell ever noticed I was in town.

I did get to know the florist, because I'd stopped by his place

100

to buy flowers for Enid Markey, and because he'd been to a preview of our show. "Ah, here she comes, the little genius," he said benevolently as I appeared.

"Never mind the applesauce—could you hear me?" I asked, since the director and I had been having a battle about volume.

"Every word," the florist said.

I strode back to the theatre, after pressing kisses on the florist's hands. "The florist heard every word," I told the director. The director (who had so many kids he'd put a restaurant milk dispenser in his kitchen, and every day you could see all the neighborhood tads lined up in front of the machine with their glasses out) didn't even flinch. "Who you going to listen to, me or the florist?" he inquired.

My go-rounds with directors have all been just about as triumphant as that.

If you're a purist, Palm Beach can't be considered the road. (The road is when you take a Broadway show, either the original company or a new company, away from Broadway and out into the country at large.) What I was doing in Palm Beach was winter stock. It's like summer stock, but it happens in the winter.

Only thing is, stock can't be considered stock anymore, if you're a purist.

Because the old stock company, where everybody worked together, and put on a different play each week, and rehearsed the next week's play in the daytimes, is pretty well dead.

The star "package" has killed it.

A package consists of a "name," which will hopefully draw the crowds, and several attendant players who travel with, and say yes to, the name. Bit parts are filled in later. They're taken by the prop boy or the manager's wife or anybody who's around the theater when the company gets there.

In a package, you go from place to place, doing the same play everywhere, holding one rehearsal in each new theatre to find out how—or if—the set is going to work, and where the lights are, and to show the local talent where they can huddle to stay out of the star's way.

A package is put together by a producer in New York (usually), who has his feet on his desk and his telephone in his hand, and who never sees what he's wrought, and who's glad of it.

He begins by getting hold of a TV personality, or a slightly over-the-hill movie star (the terrible truth is, folks, that you're never going to find Paul Newman out beating the bushes), or a good solid second banana from the movies, or a stage actor with a certain amount of prestige. Around this figure the packager builds his dream.

It's all exploitation.

On Broadway, when a new play comes along, while it's nice to have Henry Fonda in it—and he'll probably have to turn it down before an unknown gets a crack at it—the real effort is to find the right actor for the part. A package works the other way. The packager starts with an available name and finds a play said name could conceivably be crammed into (every middle-aged female ex-movie star in the world went out with *Barefoot in the Park*, every middle-aged male ex-movie star with *Never Too Late*). Then the packager contacts theatre owners across the country to see who'll buy whom. Maybe an owner would have been interested in Bert Lahr for *Never Too Late*, the year that play was covering the country, but he'd already booked Dennis O'Keefe, say, and so it goes.

The package's supporting roles are offered to actors willing to work for two hundred dollars a week so that the name can pull down his or her several grand, because it's the name who will bring in the audiences.

At each summer—or winter—stock theatre, there's a staff that does all the hard work: the set designers, the people who light, the apprentices who slave long hours for no pay because they hope to get acting parts, but who rarely get sprung from the nail bench.

Here are excerpts from a correspondence I had with an apprentice:

Excerpt 1: *"September Tide* is a cold mackerel. The ingenue is the arms-flying, windmill type, the character lady is weather-beaten, the star is playing for inner values, so inner that nothing gets over the foots."

Excerpt 2: *"Devil's Disciple* opened tonight. I hate them. I've worked forty-eight hours with seven hours' sleep. I'd quit, but I have a bit part that gasses me. I get to wear a British officer's uniform, replete with gold braid and sword. I put it on as soon as I can and stride around the shop slashing at people and screaming orders."

Excerpt 3: "I have figured out why the lighting guy married his wife. Her feet are the same size as his and she can wear his army boots."

The apprentice sees all and hears all because he has to be everywhere and do everything. He has to build sets and paint them and tear them down. By contrast, the set designer only has to design sets so they won't collapse and kill somebody—ergo, his area of interest is much narrower.

Excerpt from a set designer's letter which illustrates my point: "Next week, *Plain and Fancy*. A million sets, two buggies and a barn. I may throw myself into the electric fan."

Narrow. Very narrow. No range at all.

Sometimes a tryout of a new play will first be performed at a stock theatre. And it will last be performed at the same place.

I've done three tryouts—in Bucks County, Pennsylvania, in

103

Cincinnati, Ohio, in Palm Beach, Florida—and none of the three plays ever "came in." That means they didn't have the stuff with which to come in to Broadway, but if you'd seen the plays, you might have thought they didn't have the stuff with which to come in out of the rain.

That was not true of the one in Cincinnati. I personally *brought* that one in out of the rain. We'd been rehearsing in the shade of a big tree because the theatre was a tent, and if you tried to work inside it during the hours when the sun was shining you got fried brains.

A couple of claps of thunder sounded and I ran for a nearby toolshed.

The director followed, yelling, "Come on out—what are you afraid of?"

"Lightning," I said, crawling under a moldy velvet-covered armchair.

The director sighed and called the rest of the cast into the toolshed so we could get on with our work.

Ten minutes later, the tree which had been sheltering us was cleft in utter twain, amidst a great smell of charring.

Once again a chicken heart and a chicken liver had triumphed over the forces of nature.

Some stock theatres are lavish, some are not.

I worked in a depressed area of Pennsylvania, right in the heart of a bunch of deserted coal towns, and it was a miracle that the audiences found the theatre, since none of the actors could.

I should have suspected, back in New York, as soon as I got my instructions. They were the kind you'd give a secret agent. I was to climb aboard such and such a bus at such and such a time, and get off at a certain roadside diner. There I would be fetched by a producer's emissary. I was. And he took me straight to an apartment in a house run by a harridan who'd been the town madam back when there'd been a town. Red lights flashed all over the outside of the place, and a large bar occupied the entire ground floor. My apartment had a private bathroom, but I checked out anyway.

The playhouse was off in the middle of an abandoned amusement park. Vainly one searched for a billboard telling where our drama was going to take place. All you saw for miles and miles were signs exhorting you to "Ride the Wild Mouse."

I would have liked to ride the Wild Mouse, but he, like everything else in the area, was closed.

Maybe the most exceptional stock experience I ever had, though, was in a little seaside resort on the New Jersey coast. President Lincoln used to summer there, and I'll bet most of the old ladies still rocking on their porches knew him real well.

We were doing *Showboat* and I was the star, which gives you some idea of the company. All over town there were cardboard posters bearing the legend "Irene Kane in *Showboat*," and all over town, as I walked behind them, I could hear people saying, "Irene who?"

The night before we opened, the guy who played one of the leads got picked up in a bar on a morals charge. Opening night, the violinist started having labor pains in the pit. And Ravenal, my leading man, was a bass baritone who couldn't make the tenor notes and who bellowed like a wounded moose. In the duets I shook, fearing that we would be stoned off the stage, but Ravenal never knew there was anything askew with his effort. He blamed the horrible sounds on the orchestra, and every night he whispered to me comfortingly, "Tomorrow they'll be better."

The house where most of the actors stayed (not me; I was down at a new motel—balcony overlooking the ocean, blue princess phone, fresh-caught fish for breakfast, a bathroom a king could have held a levee in, and a bill I had to float a bank loan to pay) was short on everything. One apprentice couldn't even get a drink of water there. "The Equity people have all the cups," he told me wistfully.

My costumes included a wedding dress which the wardrobe mistress had borrowed from a local museum, and which she thrust toward me proudly. It was a rich, warm brown.

"It's brown," I said.

"It's a genuine antique," she said.

I convinced her that the gown's original wearer (Betsy Ross? Pocahontas?) wouldn't have got married in brown, and neither would I; I'd make do with a plain white shirt and a long cheese-cloth veil.

Well, I crawled out there in my cheesecloth, but the groom didn't show. Standing and waiting, I heard the wardrobe mistress in the wings. "You're wearing Ravenal's pants," she was hissing to a member of the chorus. "And he's running around in his underwear!"

Since I didn't play the guitar, I'd been promised a musician for my big nightclub scene, but the only apprentice available was just learning to chord a little. "Sing it in the key he can play it in," the management advised.

The lady enacting my mother had worse trouble. She'd spent a whole year on the road with a company of *My Fair Lady*. All the boys in the cast had been sissies, mean sissies at that. "So I finally get into a company with some men," she said, "and I go into my dressing room, and there's a fifteen-year-old girl smoking a cigar and reading *The Well of Loneliness.*"

Road or stock, the food is mostly terrible, but the only actor I ever heard about who made a first-class row over it was a chap named Felix Munso. I was not personally acquainted with Felix

106

Munso, but I read about him often because he used to be written up whenever Equity (the stage actors' union) put out its monthly magazine. The magazine printed minutes of Equity meetings and Mr. Munso went to most of the meetings and talked most of the time. Usually about abuses endured in pursuit of his muse.

He'd worked, for example, at a theatre in Westport, Connecticut, where the quality of the food furnished the actors so exercised him that he'd slung "a tuna fish sandwich into the pool."

There was considerable talk at the next Equity meeting over that. Mr. Munso had also complained about lack of proper payment by the Westport producer, and the fact that the producer's husband was "recording the performances." This, said one Equity official, "somehow gave us an impression of Mr. S—— furtively and clandestinely running a tape machine, and being surprised at it by Mr. Munso." Such an impression was incorrect, the official went on to state.

I was crazy about Mr. Munso, but in time I grew fearful that he'd had it. My fears were based on the following minutes of an Equity meeting. They concluded as follows:

"Godfrey Cambridge thanked those present 'for reaffirming my faith in my brother actors.' Felix Munso had his hand up, but the Chairman doubted the existence of a quorum. Before he could call for one, a motion to adjourn was moved and seconded."

Maybe it was only a straw in the wind, but it sounded like they were muzzling Felix at last.

Actors on the road travel a number of ways. Most stars fly first class, though Arthur and Virginia Treacher were in the habit of driving a station wagon complete with family silver, frying pans, Yorkshire terrier—the dog I knew was named Emily Treacher; she sent out Christmas cards—and framed wedding pictures of Joe E. and Mrs. Joe E. Brown. If a couple of people in a cast have cars, car pools are preferable to those Toonerville trolleys on which managements see fit to dispatch actors.

And if you're going by car, you usually travel at night. You close in a town, and the curtain's down, but you're still up. It takes time to unwind, and you'd rather drive than go to bed, so you head for the next town. And because fine French restaurants aren't open all night, you wind up eating in greasy spoons at odd hours.

There you meet other actors, a smattering of drunks, a few truckdrivers, an occasional tourist who also likes to drive in the dark. And there's something relaxed, almost giddy, about a diner at three o'clock in the morning.

I watched a cook in a tall white hat come out of his kitchen and make an impassioned speech to another man. "In my life," said the cook, "I have known too much of sorrow and bullshit."

From the booth behind me rose the voice of a sozzled lady customer. "Thass a very expressive cook," she told the waitress.

The waitress agreed. "And the person he's expressing himself to is the boss. He'll be out of work tomorrow."

Won't we all.

Hungry for ambrosia, we choke down the tuna fish Munso despises; hoping to catch the gravy train, we hitch rides on ruptured interstate buses (no spitting, no smoking, no toilet, no air) and get off at the roadside diner, on our way to the rainbow, the bluebird, the Wild Mouse.

14

An Actor Prepares to Eat: How to Keep the Mind Alive, Along with the Stomach

Guts and imagination were the two things Lee Strasberg said an actor needed.

Out of work is the one thing an actor generally gets.

And while joblessness doesn't develop guts—at least in me it hasn't—it does confer upon the actor that leisure in which to develop his imagination.

At one time I had so many creative thoughts I considered going into business with them. Some actors walk dogs or sling hash. I've already told how I chose letters for an advice column. But that old lady's advice column wasn't enough to keep the mind alive, let alone the stomach, and then I got this other idea about selling my creative thoughts. I decided I could liven up cocktail parties. Either in person, by hiring out to appear at parties and tell lies, or by peddling lies to such avid party-goers as might be willing to pay for them.

Lies about foreign travel was the area I resolved to concentrate on, because these days everybody travels and your having been to Florence is no longer enough to make your neighbors' eyes pop. Now a funny thing has to happen to you on the way to the Duomo.

So I created a bunch of fantastic adventures, guaranteed to

make the reputation of any reveler, even some gringo who's never been south of Washington Square.

But nobody bought them. Or me. Now I'm wondering if I was thinking too small. Maybe I should have offered them as movie ideas to Orson Welles or Alfred Hitchcock, men who appreciate lyricism, tenderness and truly fine plots.

I would be willing to collaborate in the filming of these superb fantasies if the producer felt my participation necessary for getting at the inner truths. Here is a sample of my work:

THE CABBAGES AND KINGS ADVENTURE
Scene: London.

I had gone to Harrods to enquire (that's the English way of doing things) if they had instant plum pudding, when I was struck by a feeling of two eyes burning into my shoulder blades. I turned and saw a sandy-haired young man shambling about, gazing at me as though his dog had died. I thought of scolding him for his forwardness, but he looked so pitiable I didn't have the heart. He asked me if I would come take tea with him and his mum, and I said to myself, "My dear, here is your chance to visit with some typically English people."

Unfortunately, there was nothing typical about them. They lived in a castle (the name of which I am not at liberty to divulge), and Bonny Prince ———, for that was his title (his Christian name I am not at liberty to divulge), took me in through some kind of a back way. Of course his mother didn't know we were coming, so she didn't have her crown on, but the tea was lovely. If you like tea.

Later Bonny P. took me home and asked me to be his. "I must 'ave yer," he said.

I drew back. "Bonny," I said, "forget it. Prince," I said,

110

"you've got all that royalty and I am the most common sort of clay; this type of a liaison would bring naught but grief to your peoples."

"I am speaking of marriage," says Bonny P., rearing up with a ferocious expression on his face. It made me nervous, knowing the blood of Henry VIII ran in his veins. "I will find it impossible," says he, "to carry on the heavy burden of responsibility and to discharge my duties as king as I would wish to do without the help and support of the woman I love."

"Support?" I said gently. "No, Bonny," I said. "I couldn't support you for a minute. Look how you live. Plus I am an American, and must return to my native land."

I am sorry to say that tears gushed from the royal orbs in a most un-English way. But I felt I was right, that our love could never be, and that someday he would thank me for this. "I feel I am right," I said, "that our love can never be, and that someday you will thank me for this."

Then I went back to Harrods. Do you know they don't have instant plum pudding?

THE WHO IS SYLVIA? WHAT IS SHE? ADVENTURE
Scene: Buenos Aires.

I had gone to Argentina to get the roses back in these cheeks, and to brush up on my carioca. By exploiting the peasants, I was able to rent a villa outside the city for a few pesos a day. My place had a tiled swimming pool, a view of the sea and an ancient crone of a maid who did all the cooking, cleaning, gardening, shopping and hemstitching. This maid dressed in black robes, with a black mantilla over her head, and she told me to call her Sylvia. She lived above the garage in which she kept her jeep. It seemed to me unusual that this poor creature should

111

own wheels, but I put suspicion out of my mind. If I had been going to be suspicious of Sylvia, I would have had many reasons besides her jeep. To be sure, certain ladies have mustaches, but Sylvia's was really bushy, and she spoke in a very queer way for a Spaniard.

When she wanted to tell me dinner was on the table, for instance, she would call hysterically, *"Kommen Sie hier,"* and believe me, I would *Kommen* right away.

Thinking she must at the very least have mixed blood, I decided to test her knowledge of pure Castilian Spanish such as I had been taught in Forest Hills High School.

"Esto es un lápiz," I said, pointing to a pencil.

Sylvia bared her teeth and growled. *"Esto es un Bleistift!"*

Mixed blood. No question.

Her cooking was strange too. In a country where one expected to find *mole* sauce, Sylvia mostly prepared *bratwurst,* and when I asked for wine of the countryside, she brought me pitchers of beer.

I tried to give her as few orders as possible, because when one did make a request of her, she had a disconcerting habit of clicking her heels together, while her right arm shot convulsively toward the roof. Her taste in music was not for boleros or fandangos either. Every night as I lay in bed I would hear "The Ride of the Valkyries" booming down from the room over the garage. One night I crept out to beg her, for heaven's sake, to turn the volume down a bit. I had never been to her digs before and when Sylvia finally opened the door (her mantilla askew) I noticed that she kept a large picture of a blond lady hanging on one wall. It was inscribed, "With love, Eva," but I am enough of a student of Argentine history to tell anyone who's interested that the blond lady was *not* Evita Peron.

Eventually, finding I could get no sleep in that place due to

Sylvia's penchant for music, I returned to the States. Here, in peace and quiet, I have been mulling things over, and I have come to the conclusion that Sylvia misrepresented herself. I believe she was actually some famous missing person. Judge Crater, perhaps.

THE LIBERTY AND JUSTICE FOR ALL ADVENTURE
Scene: Tel Aviv.

Only a few moments earlier I had left the King David Hotel and was walking down a broad, pleasant boulevard flanked by dill pickle trees when I bumped into two screaming women. They were pulling each other's hair and calling each other names, and there was a baby sitting in a basket watching them and laughing. It developed that each of these women—and may I say neither of them looked as though she were any better than she should be—was claiming to be the mother of the infant.

In a flash I was inspired to see how I could settle the entire nastiness. I whipped out my Swiss Red Cross knife (which includes a compass, a can opener, a pair of scissors, a screwdriver, a corkscrew, a file, a leather punch, a small blade and a long blade) and I brandished it before those startled women. "I am going to split that laughing baby right down the middle," I said, "and give each of you one half."

The first woman took this judgment hard. "Bad scene," she shouted. "Don't you dare carve that chile with no Swiss Red Cross knife. That whoo-er can have him."

The second woman was unmoved. "It all right with me, whatever you do, jes' so's I git my cut," she said.

Instantly I knew she was not the mother. I picked up the baby and the basket and presented them to the first woman, and suddenly I found myself the center of a milling crowd, all discussing my sapience. They carried me on their shoulders to a courthouse and proclaimed me a circuit judge. I refused the honor, with thanks. Because while I take a stab at it now and again, wisdom isn't my game.

THE DEADLY PIGEON ADVENTURE
Scene: Venice.

I had occasion to try and save America recently. At least I think it was America, but it may have been some other country. The way it began, I was traveling to Venice, city of intrigue, in a third-class carriage, when I met a man who offered to show me around as soon as we arrived. This troubled me vaguely since it was 3 A.M., and I was of the opinion that no museums would be open.

As we stepped off the train into the *vaporetto,* the ticket taker, indicating my suitcase, spoke, *sotto voce,* to my companion. "The bag," he said, "travels as a person."

My companion explained that I had to pay a fare for my bag, but I knew there was more to it. Any seasoned reader of spy stories could have told as much. (Let me add, I am *not* a fanciful person.) Plain though it was that I had walked into a mess which might have international ramifications, fatigue caused me to let down my guard. Arriving at my *pensione,* I went to bed and spent the night in fitful sleep.

Next morning, eager to take a previously arranged Cook's tour, I approached a bellboy. *"Dove* Cook's?" I inquired.

Without a moment's hesitation, he directed me toward a pair of swinging doors at the rear of the dining room. I had evidently —and inadvertently—hit upon a password. My forebodings of the prior evening returned tenfold, but there was nothing to do except play the game out. I opened the doors.

114

In the kitchen, for such the place was, I found two men talking. "The secret of the pigeon is in seventy-five minutes at three hundred fifty degrees," one said to the other.

The moment they looked up, I fled. I had to get back to my room and sort it all out. Pigeon. Wasn't "pigeon" a key word in the argot of the underworld? Directly I went to the slang dictionaries I carry everywhere. A pigeon, said the first, was "anyone hastening with news surreptitiously." Of course. A dead pigeon, said the second, was "anyone faced with imminent or unavoidable disaster." The third was even more ominous. It indicated that "to fly a blue pigeon" meant "to steal lead off a church."

My heart pounded. Church. *San Marco?* I raced to the *piazza*. No one trying to steal lead so far as I could see. Then it hit me. There must have been a thousand pigeons in the great square, but which of them was "hastening with news surreptitiously"? The guilty carrier, around whose leg the fateful clue must be banded, was somewhere in the mob. Three hundred fifty degrees, the conspirators had said. But were they talking latitude? Longitude?

I sat down in a café chair and waited seventy-five minutes. Several times I was approached by a single pigeon. He would come to within a few steps of me, then, seeming to change his mind, would hasten away.

Desperate now, I sought out the police. They, too, were deep in the plot; they tried to tell me those conspirators in the kitchen had been chefs discussing the preparation of squabs. What did they take me for? I wondered.

American Express was my last hope. I rushed to the office. There a young man with hooded eyes passed on to me the following intelligence. "Your Cook's tour has been canceled," he said meaningfully, "but we have substituted a visit to the island of Murano, where you will watch men blowing glass."

115

I went limp with relief. Obviously my stumbling into their intrigue had caused its perpetrators to cancel the pigeon caper. Now I could leave Venice with an easy mind. Still, Murano, Murano . . . It has a sinister sound.

THE INCREDIBLE TWINKLETOES ADVENTURE
Scene: Moscow.

It happened while I was standing on line outside the theatre, hoping to get a ticket for the Bolshoi Ballet. The day was perishing cold, and I was hopping from one foot to another and beating my hands together, trying to keep from being frozen to death by the very Russian winter which had defeated Napoleon. (Not the *very* winter, of course; creative artists are permitted this type of poetic license.) I did not notice two men in fur hats sobbing and gesticulating until they were almost upon me.

"Sahm cute-nitz," said one.

The other nodded. "Is clearly top-drawer stuff."

Over my violent protests, they pulled me out of line and dragged me around the corner, assuming the conspiratorial attitude I recognized from seeing Russians in the movies. There, in a subway kiosk, while balalaikas played, they told me their story. They were in charge of the ballet, and tonight the entire Politburo was coming to the opening of *Swan Lake,* and the prima ballerina had been took bad. All the other prima ballerinas were on vacation, so there was no one to replace her, and these fellows were going to lose their jobs, their apartments in town, their dachas in the country, and have to go to work, if *Swan Lake* didn't go on as scheduled.

I agreed that things looked awful for them, but what did they want of me?

"Do it again," the first one said.

116

"Do what again?" I asked.

"Dot leetle dense," he said. "Vair you hop from wan foo to dahther."

Under stress, his accent was growing worse.

"Da, da," said the second man. "Ahnd you bit yure leetle hahnds togadder."

He didn't sound like James Mason either.

"But it wasn't a dance," I told them shyly, and explained about Americans having iron-poor blood, and the devices we had to stoop to in order to keep it circulating. I admitted I had done a little dancing back in grammar school—polka, time step, the usual.

They begged me to help them out. "You got natchell rim," they said. "You sving."

You've probably guessed the end. I agreed to appear—incognito—for the ballerina. I wouldn't be announced; I'd just go out and do my thing and save these comrades' skins.

But on my own terms. At my first entrance, I insisted, the orchestra must switch from Tchaikovsky to an American composer, and play "Three Cheers for the Jones Junior High" (or "Stars and Stripes Forever," as it is sometimes called), whereupon I would break into my justly famous military toe tap.

All went as planned. No sooner had I executed the first brush, brush, step than the audience started to pelt me—with roses, with caviar, with vodka (some still in the bottles), with lettuce and mixed fruits and such noise as I have never heard before. If I had understood the language, I could tell you better of my triumph.

117

15

Elementary Lessons in Television

Having already revealed so many top acting secrets, I'm tired. But conscience presses me forward because I am aware that some of you want to know how to get big in television. I am now addressing those for whom the legitimate theatre is not a viable answer. (The question doesn't signify. Either you got too soft of a voice, or eating every couple days means something to you, or just your feet get hot pounding the pavements, as we say on the Great White Way.) So television is more like your natural habitat.

I will now disseminate everything I know about television, and if you put it in your left eye, you will still be able to see very good.

My first job in television was on a show called "Studio One." I played a little girl dying of consumption. She was a bareback rider in a circus. The star of the show was Cathleen Nesbitt, who played the operator of a theatrical boardinghouse. I got the job at the last minute because the girl the "Studio One" people wanted left town suddenly, and I was in the office when she told the casting people to take their part and stuff it.

I showed up at the rehearsal hall down on lower Second Avenue, and a big-wheel agent from Music Corporation of America greeted me, and I thought, Boy, I'm somebody. Then I found out the agent was there because Cathleen Nesbitt had forgotten her glasses and somebody'd had to fetch them down.

Lesson 1: If you want the keys to the city, marry the mayor.

I played a Southern waif in one episode of a series called "The House on High Street," and when it showed, Enid Markey called me up crying, she was so moved. So I tried to buy a copy of the tape in order to keep a record of my greatness. But the people in charge of tapes had erased it.

Lesson 2: Greatness isn't always apparent to anyone but Enid Markey.

I was in the pilot for "The Defenders" series, which pilot featured Steve McQueen. "Look at him," said a character lady. "He looks just like a monkey." But when it came time for lightning to strike, it didn't touch the character lady or me; it traveled right around us and hit Simian McQueen.

Lesson 3: Too much beauty can be a handicap.

I did a "Naked City" back when the only costumes "Naked City" had on hand were cops' uniforms, and I was sent out shopping with the wardrobe man, a sweet old guy who wasn't used to procuring clothing for girls. The director had told him to buy me a bouffant party dress. We went to Lord & Taylor, me in blue jeans, him in lumber jacket and hearing aid, and when a saleslady asked us what we wanted—they'd never seen anything like us in Lord & Taylor—the old guy told her. "One of them buffoon dresses," he said.

Lesson 4: "Clothes makes the man." I'm not sure what Lesson 4 means, but my grandma always said it.

I played a juvenile delinquent in a "My True Story" melodrama, and I hit an elderly man on the head with the butt of

119

a gun. My little nephew saw it and after that, whenever I came to his house he burst into tears and hid in a closet.

Lesson 5: Kids are stupid.

Once I sang "Bye, Bye, Blackbird" on a television variety show.

Once I acted a scene from an off-Broadway play on another television variety show.

I wasn't asked back by either variety show.

Lessons 6 and 7: Money spent on singing teachers and member-ship in a Variety Guild is money wasted.

Actually, I met a dog named Harrison who worked on television more than I did. He was a Yorkie, and his owner wasn't entirely thrilled with his stardom. "The agent calls and says, 'Is Harrison available?'" she complained. "Why doesn't he call and ask if *I'm* available to take the dog to the audition?"

Lesson 8: Four legs are better than two, especially if you can grow fur on them.

Harrison mostly did commercials, because to make a living in New York in television, there are only two ways you can go—commercials and/or soap operas.

Commercials were never my form of expression. I tried three times. The first time I was supposed to smear soap on my face and then look lovingly at the radiant new me in the mirror.

I got the soap on my face, but then I couldn't stop laughing.

The second time I was supposed to be an airline stewardess and help carry a baby off a plane for a lady passenger. I was handed the baby (a wrapped-up towel—there wasn't even a doll in it) and when I got to the bottom of the ramp I hurled it at the camera. Don't ask me why I did it. A manic need to go hungry is the best reason I can come up with.

120

And those two times were actual jobs; the third time was only an audition.

The third time, the casting director didn't even bother to come into the office with the candidates to listen to how they did. She just handed each applicant a mimeographed sheet, the contents of which the applicant was supposed to read into a tape recorder. After laying the material on the actor, she would point him toward an empty cubicle. "In there," she'd say. "Slate yourself and go right into copy."

A friend explained to me what this meant, and when my turn came I reverted to total adolescent. I shut the cubicle door behind me and addressed the tape machine. "Mrs. Leslie Carter," I said. "Take One."

I don't know about commercials. Maybe if you could get one of the great ones—"Here's news for hemorrhoid sufferers"; "a pretty face, but oh, that midriff bulge"; even "the heartbreak of psoriasis"—it would be worth hanging around ad agencies half your life.

But I don't think so.

Which may only mean that I draw my lines in funny places. Because while I scoff at commercials, I cherish the most tender of feelings for soap operas, an art form scorned by many.

Not by my grandma, though. My grandma had lived several soap operas, and listened to many more, back in the days of radio. The daily listening had left her with a strange affliction of speech; often she talked just like a soap opera.

Take the time Ma Perkins was residing on a houseboat and a storm pulled her out to sea. Luckily her son the sailor was visiting, and he was able to steer the whole establishment back to safe harbor. "Though he was but a simple gob," Grandma observed.

If you came to my grandma's apartment while Portia was

facing life, Grandma would hiss, "Shh," even though she had the sound up so loud on that wireless set she'd bought from the Victor Talking Machine Company that you could feel the vibrations in Jersey City. And my grandma lived in Brooklyn.

Grandma not only talked *like* the shows, she talked *at* the shows. If a hussy announced that she was planning to lure Lord Henry Brinthrope, "England's richest and most handsome peer," away from Our Gal Sunday, "an orphan girl from the little mining town of Silver Creek, Colorado," Grandma wheeled toward the radio, teeth bared. "That's what you think, you damn fool!" she snarled.

And when Helen Trent (of "The Romance of Helen Trent") was chatting with a stranger and revealing far too much, my grandmother shook her head gloomily. "Little does she know," said Grandma, "that she's speaking to a detective."

Little did my grandma know that I would grow up to be a famous soap opera star and bring honor and glory to my family.

Or at least that I'd get a couple years' work on "Love of Life." *Lesson 9: Even your grandma don't know everything.*

16

Here on the Edge of Night, as I Searched for Tomorrow, I Found Love of Life

I got on "Love of Life" when a casting lady saw my picture in *Players' Guide.* (*Players' Guide* is a book you pay nine dollars a year to have your picture in, so Federico Fellini will spot you and cable your agent, "Attza one I gotta have it.")

The casting lady sent me to read for Larry Auerbach, the director, who hired me, and I hung around for the better part of three years, playing Connie Loomis, a lion-hearted high school dropout. (This was back in the sixties, when life was simple. So was Connie Loomis.)

Rosehill, Connie's hometown, was a small community which managed to support a gambling casino, an international financier and one family of shiftless ne'er-do-wells. Hers.

Ah, Connie, I remember you in your flower, bravely laughing off the disgrace of having the town drunk for a father, earnestly trying to persuade your rotten brother Frankie to throw his gat in the river, virtuously snatching your little tail from out of the grasp of that sleazy hotel manager in the mountains.

You were okay, Con. Even when Alan Sterling, son of the town's leading family, got a crush on you, you didn't behave like the floozies on soaps do nowadays—get pregnant and expect him to marry you. All you did was hack around. (Whatever that

123

meant. Every time anyone on the show asked, "What were you and Alan doing, Connie?" you would say, "Aw, hackin' around.") But when you gave your lower-class heart, it was to Tony Vento, who worked in a garage. Tony's mother, Mrs. Vento, was a cleaning woman. You could tell by the way she never went anyplace without her pail. She wore a little porkpie straw hat that looked just like Charley Weaver's, and she wore it summer, winter, spring and fall, indoors and out. The Ventos were your kind of folks.

Enough of sentimental wallowing, however. Readers probably want to know hard facts about what it's like to be an idol of the American television-viewing public.

It's terrific. Once you're in a soap, the American television-viewing public can't do enough for you. They point at you in buses, they greet you in department stores (always by your character name; they know little and care less about your real name), they try to help you across the street.

I was in a play with Peggy McCay, who'd been "Love of Life" 's original leading lady, Vanessa Dale Raven Sterling, and Peggy said good samaritans had constantly accosted her on Lexington Avenue to whisper, "Dear, your sister isn't really crippled. When you leave the room, she gets out of that wheelchair and walks." After a while, Peggy learned to say, "Thanks. I'll surely look into that."

If you're a soap opera performer who takes a leave of absence in order to do some other kind of show, every second stranger you meet will try to catch you up on what's happened with your soap while you've been gone.

In Las Vegas, the girl who straightened my hotel room out also straightened me out. And she talked just like my grandma while she was doing it. "Dr. Saltzman," she said, "has declared his love, but I fear it is Vanessa who will be hurt."

124

It isn't just when they meet one in person that the American television-viewing public shows its idols how it feels. Idols hear by mail and phone too.

My telephone-answering service, for instance, was addicted to "Love of Life." (I was relieved to discover this, because I'd always wondered what my telephone-answering service did all day. God knows it didn't answer my telephone.)

Each time I got back to my apartment from "Love of Life," the answering service would ring up with notes and comment: "Bus line looked beautiful today." Bus line? I'd *walked* home from the garage. Continuing, the conversation became clearer. My service was trying to buck me up about my *poitrine*. "You pretty, Connie. You just *think* you ain't."

With a service like that, who needs a mommy?

Once a call came to the studio from a guy who said he was a big Hollywood director phoning person to person from California, he knew quality when he saw it, and he was going to fly me to the moon. Then the operator told him to drop in another nickel.

(I was at CBS when an employee had to deal with an irate viewer who'd dialed the station in the middle of "Twilight Zone." The viewer said she'd turned her back for a minute and the spooks had come out of the set and stolen her pocketbook. She wanted to know what CBS was going to do about it. Television networks are used to screwy calls.)

And them as don't phone write.

Even the mighty keep in touch. P. G. Wodehouse wrote to tell us he always stopped whatever he was doing at noon in order to watch "Love of Life." And our entire cast was summoned to a party laid on by a Park Avenue baron and baroness. We got a letter saying we'd given the baron and baroness "such pleasant entertainment that they wish to reciprocate."

It was some evening. The baroness took me aside and told me she'd outlived six husbands. Then the baron took me aside and told me she wasn't going to outlive *him.*

Well, I said to myself, that's rich people for you, and fell onto the pâté. (There is nothing an actor won't eat if it's free. The late Preston Sturges once told me he'd had so much trouble with a movie banquet scene during the course of which the extras kept wolfing the props that he'd had all the food sprayed with lacquer. The extras ate it anyway.)

Getting back to mail, though, I am in possession of one remarkable epistle sent airmail special delivery from a lady in California. After "Love of Life" killed off a sympathetic character named Maggie (it was a long, lingering death which took about a year, and Lord, how the ratings shot up), the show brought Maggie's wicked twin sister, Kay, into the plot to try to seduce Maggie's bereaved husband, Link. The California lady became frantic.

"Link thought he was in the clouds with his dead wife," she wrote. "But Kay does not look like Maggie at all as Maggie had black hair and brown eyes and wouldn't *hurt any one.* Link, you forgot you were on CBS-TV coast to coast. Three million people saw everything."

That California lady had spied Link kissing Kay, and she was sore as a pup. "Link was on TV every day, and is still on TV. Kay don't love him. She plans to spend all his money. She is in love with a New York man. If Link would tune in his TV, he would know all this. He is surely out of his mind."

The letter was signed, "Mrs. Brown, a trained nurse."

Not only the fans but the actors lose touch with reality. They begin to think they're indispensable. Sad to say, they're not. More than ten years ago, "Love of Life" 's leading man went to

126

bed on a Thursday night with one Vanessa and rose on Friday morning with an entirely different girl. Thursday's Van had asked the producer for more money.

"Love of Life" is now owned outright by CBS, but in those days the producer was a man named Roy Winsor. And Roy Winsor must have been a lot like Sam Levenson's mother. Remember Sam Levenson's mother, when one of her kids threatened to leave home? "Go," she'd say. "I'll make you sandwiches." Well, when an actor threatened to quit a Roy Winsor soap if he didn't get more money, Roy Winsor headed straight for the Tasty bread.

Winsor also used to produce "The Secret Storm" (which was to have been called "The Storm Within" before an antacid sponsor picked it up) and he let its star go in an argument over cash. Actor Peter Hobbs had been playing character Peter Ames for eight years, yet Winsor was unconcerned. "In a daytime serial," he said, "the character is certainly more important than the actor."

The outraged Hobbs gave an interview listing the various sufferings he'd endured as Peter Ames, and he sounded as though he'd got Hobbs and Ames so mixed up he himself couldn't tell the difference anymore. "My wife died in the first episode, and I was left to raise three children," he said, pondering Winsor's ingratitude. "Since then there's been a juvenile delinquency problem, a school problem, a new wife, mother-in-law trouble . . ."

You think it's easy raising a crowd of motherless kids? Without money?

I never met Roy Winsor. But I never asked for a raise either. I thought I was overpaid. I would come in at eight in the morning for makeup, costume, rehearsal, go on camera at noon, and be back on Fifty-eighth Street by twelve-thirty, a couple of hundred dollars richer and free to go walking in Central Park. It was paradise enow.

Of course there were hazards in live television. The day I had to cut a cake on air, a prop man had thoughtfully frozen it solid "so it wouldn't get sour." And the day I had to eat a sandwich on air, the director sent a fellow out to get "anything but peanut butter," but all the fellow heard was "peanut butter," so I told my troubles to Vanessa while sounding as though I'd left my dentures home.

But mostly it was swell. I was far-sighted (which meant I could read the Teleprompter if I got into trouble, and didn't have to go around writing my lines all over the furniture and the floor as some soap actors do) and I was crazy about the director, who was funny, smart, never mean. Even when the absent-minded boy who played Tony Vento wandered away after dress rehearsal under the impression that he'd done the air show (eventually he wandered clear to California and never came back) and the world was treated to a blank screen and organ music while the stage manager tracked Tony down, Larry stayed cool. Even when, twenty minutes before air time, a character woman went dry on every one of her speeches, Larry stayed kind. "Dear," he said mildly, "I know there are certain things better left unsaid—but *all* of them?"

And I was even crazier about the stage manager than I was about the director. The stage manager had red hair, a permanent cold in the head, he dressed as bad as Howard Hughes, and he'd spent a year working for the unfailingly gentle Captain Kangaroo. This had left him with a compulsion to kick a lamb whenever he saw one (fortunately, few lambs hung out on Fifty-eighth Street) and a habit of going around the studio singing, "Quack, quack, quadackus, said the little red hen." But he was

128

beautiful in his Bakelite earmuffs, flapping his newspaper to cue us into a scene, and when he invited me on a short cruise—he was taking the ferry to Staten Island—I realized Connie Loomis had met her match.

What did I get out of "Love of Life"? My husband the stage manager, twenty-six weeks of unemployment compensation when the gig was over, and the simple adoration of the American television-viewing public, which still comes up to me and asks, "Hey, are you anybody?"

17

My Last Crack at Television Luminariness, or "It's Your Move, Baby," He Said

In the summer of '72, my husband Mike, the stage manager, turned into a big television producer. He told me so himself. "Stick with me, baby," he said, "and it'll be T-bones right up to your tiara."

I said I was more spiritual than that. "Even better," he said. "I got you a job don't pay a nickel, but you'll bring happiness to countless thousands." Then he put me on a Trailways bus and took me to Albany.

You probably didn't know that most of the important television in the country comes from Albany. I didn't either, until I got caught in the middle of the world chess championship match.

It began because New York City's Channel 13, WNET, had unprogramed air time in the summer afternoons. And because my husband runs what is called an educational television network. (You must have seen some of the wonderful work they put on. Who else gives you a close look at gum surgery? Just as you're sitting down to dinner?)

And because they were both chess freaks, my husband and a Channel 13 vice-president, Frank Leicht, decided it would be nice to cover the Bobby Fischer–Boris Spassky chess games.

They made deals to get the moves wired from Iceland, and another chess freak, who was going over for the match, promised he'd phone them with rich, warm human-interest stories.

"How much are you paying him?" I asked my husband.

"Whaddya mean, paying him?" said my husband. "He loves chess."

"You don't think it's naïve," I said, "to assume some man is going to go to Iceland at his own expense to tell you if Bobby Fischer sleeps in pajamas?"

"I see what you mean," said my husband. "We'll try to get him fifty bucks a week."

Mike's choice for the star of Channel 13's "World Championship Chess" was a sad-eyed chess master named Shelby Lyman, a fixture at New York's Marshall Chess Club. Shelby, who'd never been on television, was going to post the moves on a king-sized board as they came in from Iceland, and then vamp till ready, analyzing the last moves until the next ones arrived.

There was no reason for Mike to assume that Shelby Lyman could do what Shelby Lyman subsequently did. All Mike knew about Shelby was that his work was teaching chess, and his hobby was buying country property with strangers, fighting with the strangers, and selling the property. At a loss.

But as an entrepreneur, Mike is fearless. (He once led a tall effete actor—dressed in Bermuda shorts and dragging a poodle on a leash—all over New York, trying to raise money to star the tall effete actor in *King Lear*.)

This time Mike's gamble paid off. Nobody told Shelby it wasn't possible to spend six or seven hours a day, for a minimum of three days a week, talking on camera; as long as Shelby didn't find out, Frank Leicht and my husband were in business.

Because I owned a yellow Dynel wig and a navy blue nylon skirt that, like Shelby's black funeral director's suit, knew the

131

way to Albany by themselves, the big boys offered me a three-times-a-week spot, too, but I was afraid of so much sudden glory.

"I'll do it Sundays," I said. "The rest of the week I'll stay home and feed the fish and try to remain humble."

We started in Albany (which is where we could get a studio cheap) early in July. Earlier than Bobby Fischer started in Iceland, if you want the truth of it. We went to Albany, but Bobby stayed on Long Island talking about money. He's not so spiritual as I.

On the Fourth of July, my husband was to bring the first game to the waiting audience. At that point, we figured it consisted of Mike's mother (if she could persuade the educational station in Denver to take the thing) and Frank's kids (who would lose their allowances if they didn't watch).

The opening game was canceled. "Do something," my husband said to me. "I don't know a rook from a handsaw," I said. "I'm going home." My husband pointed out that I didn't have the $7.50 Trailways would require, and that he would abandon me in Albany, to turn into one of those old folks who scrounge around in garbage pails, unless I pitched in and helped fill some of that empty air time. So I wrote a little piece about Independence Day, and how we in the U.S. had the rockets' red glare, and in Iceland we just had the Reds glaring, and I went on camera and shared these deep thoughts with the world, and the magnetism of my presence was so strong that everybody who tuned in called up. "Why did you broadcast if there wasn't any game?" they wanted to know.

On July 6, still lacking a game, we did it again. This time I wrote a piece comparing Fischer to chess geniuses Morphy and Steinitz. Shelby's wet eyes overflowed. "That's wicked," he said. Morphy and Steinitz had been crazy, Bobby was not. Okay, I said, and wrote a piece comparing Fischer to chess geniuses

132

Capablanca and Marshall. I didn't know one from another; I got all my information by eavesdropping.

On Wednesday, July 11, there *was* a game, and not only did the moves shoot in from Iceland, but Shelby was brilliant, lyrical, endearingly dopey. If he heard a voice from the control room in his ear, he looked up, startled, and answered back, for all the world like Joan of Arc, and often he tried, on a dead phone, to rouse a fellow master at the Marshall Chess Club in Manhattan ("Hello? Hello, Edmar? Are you there, Edmar?").

As the games went on, Shelby got smoother, everybody settled down, and the match became a rage, a fad, a hit show. Every day the switchboards at Channel 13 lit up with people trying to help Bobby Fischer make his next move. Reviewers were saying it was great entertainment—one guy called it "addictive"—and people who didn't play, or understand, chess watched it anyway.

Little girls baked cookies for Shelby, and I took the eye of many a television columnist. What wouldn't a girl give for a notice which read: "Sometimes the producer's wife comes on and acts as host." And if that M.C. Pig columnist wasn't bad enough, a woman I hadn't seen in ten years phoned to tell me she was wild about the show and that there was a sensational girl on it. "She has this funny little face," the woman said.

I thought about this. "Is she wearing a horsehair wig with bangs?" I said. "Yes," she said. "It's me," I said. "Oh," she said, confused. "Have you got a funny little face?"

Well, yeah, you could say that. Though it makes me want to strike back savagely.

We whiled away the summer with Boris and Bobby, in the dead city of Albany, a block away from Governor Rockefeller's great marble mall which seems to commemorate the city's demise. (Downtown Albany doesn't even have a movie house

anymore, and the rooms in the once proud De Witt Clinton—
a hotel that rolled out a strip of red carpet back when Lucky
Lindy came to spend the night—smell of dust and gasoline.)
And when it was over, America had a new champ, Bobby
Fischer. And a new television personality. Right. Shelby Ly-
man.

18

Grandma Was a Regular Sarah Heartburn

I mentioned that my grandmother talked like a soap opera, but that doesn't really tell it about my grandmother. And maybe I should tell it about her, because she's the reason I listed toward the stage.

She was a large woman, and a strong taste (some people, particularly daughters-in-law, never acquired it), and she was a ham from her pale-blue eyes right down to her hocks. I once heard a lady describe her daughter as "a regallah Sarah Heartburn"; that description would have fit my grandmother.

She was born in Germany, spent the first five years of her life in London, then emigrated to America. I bet they had to let her steer the boat.

Her gift for hyperbole heightened the events of my everyday life, and though I was her favorite, she was by no means indiscriminately sentimental about her relatives. Once, after my father and my uncle had come and gone, leaving birthday presents, she held up my uncle's offering and sniffed. "With the mother," she said, "he's a two-dollar man." And when that uncle's son got married, Grandma kept quiet until the young couple produced their second baby. Then she issued an ultimatum. "I can't buy baby gifts," she said, "if they're going to breed like flies."

Saturday afternoons, regardless of war, sleet, or crises in the family, my grandmother would take me out for a Chinese lunch. She called all the waiters Max, and she never left more than a dime tip. When I got old enough, I'd sneak back to the table and put down more money, and she'd follow me and swipe what I'd put down.

Later we'd sit at the movies, sobbing through the sad parts, and we'd go home purified.

My grandmother was a mistress of melodrama (a foghorn wailing through the night was said by her to be "calling" someone to a well-deserved punishment, such as death in the electric chair for rudeness), and though I was only six years old when I had my tonsils out, the version of my operation enacted by my grandmother stays with me still, when more logical scenes have fled my mind.

"That butcher had the knife in his hand," she said, "and the blood was gushing, and suddenly they all knelt down in the middle of the operation, the doctor and the nurses and everybody, and they prayed. There was nothing else they could do." Think of it. All those incompetents quitting cold, not even bothering to stanch the blood, depending on prayer to get them through their tonsillectomies, and perhaps a few house calls. For years I reveled in that spectacle, starring my small stricken self.

Skilled in the ancient art of vapors, when Grandma wanted to get your serious attention, she looked around for a soft chair, backed up to it, announced, "I'm going to faint dead away," and keeled over. She never fell on anything sharp, and one of her eyes remained ajar to record the impression she was making, but she terrorized both her sons, and broke up any number of romances, marriages and conversations by the ferocity of her swooning.

136

I never knew my grandfather, a small man who'd died before I was born, eroded, so they told me, by life with that fine fierce woman. Her stories about her husband were tinged with a kind of affectionate contempt.

"We had a new horse," she'd say, beginning one of her histrionic accounts. "A bay." (They'd lived in Binghamton, New York, and owned a general store, which she'd run, while he'd been sent to do errands and collect eggs from farms around the countryside. He was no good for collecting money; he was too soft.) "And he took this brand-new horse out on a hot August day," she'd go on. "And I said to him, 'Mr. G., don't let the horse get overheated. But if the horse does get overheated, don't let him drink any water.'" Short pause, to permit Stanislavski's "given circumstances" to sink in. Then: "Well," she'd say, "the horse did get overheated, and they stopped at a stream, and that horse drank some water and turned around three times and fell down dead."

Long pause. And finally Grandma's voice, world weary, would drop the curtain. "All my life, I worked and slaved to pay for dead horses."

I always wanted to applaud when she was finished.

Before she had me to work on, Grandma had struggled to make a dramatic *artiste* out of her only daughter by giving her "elocution" lessons. Thereafter, Grandma said, the girl had caused a sensation at a Masons meeting, reciting an epic poem called "The Soul of Eileen." My father says the poem was really called "The Soul of a Violin," and Grandma clearly hadn't understood a word of it.

Grandma liked rhetorical questions which she herself could answer without pausing for breath. If, for instance, she had been stood up by a plumber, the speech would go, "He was supposed to come at ten o'clock. You seen him? So did I!"

She also liked the funny papers in the New York *Daily News*. Daddy Warbucks was her idol, and she worried until the day she died about Winnie Winkle's missing husband.

For years she lived in an apartment in Brooklyn, and when she was too feeble to keep house anymore, and they moved her to a nursing home on a beautiful green street in Forest Hills, she was furious. "It's boring," she said. "Now, from *my* apartment, I'd look out the window, I'd see a hippie, I'd see a dog . . ."

I keep remembering her in that Brooklyn window toward the end of her life, half hidden in the dusk behind her rows of scabby plants, and no lights on. She was saving electricity, the way old people sometimes do. It isn't just the loneliness of those twilights that hurts, but the loss of vigor implicit in them, the realization that the once-proud tartar had nobody to fight anymore. There were no young daughters-in-law left to challenge, no waiters to outwit, no horses to protect; the battles, won or lost, were over.

She left me a thousand dollars, scraped together out of pennies saved by sitting in the dark.

19

You Can't Make Anomaly Without Breaking Eggs

I overheard a guy talking very grandly about a fund-raising gala. "It'll be on a voluntary basis," he said. "Whom goes and whom does not go."

With actors, it's just the opposite. Whom eats and whom does not eat is largely involuntary, so actors have a preoccupation with food.

"There is no greater anomaly in nature than a bird that cannot fly," Darwin tells us. Unless it is an actor that cannot eat.

And we all know you can't make anomaly without breaking eggs.

Eggs are very important to an actor, since they can sustain his life. Learning to cook is very important to an actor, too, once he has wearied of tuna straight from the can.

Tragically, I've never had a deep understanding of cooking. When I was a child, my mother, reading a recipe aloud, asked me to bring her "butter the size of an egg," and I fetched an egg with the sides nicely buttered.

I couldn't even get fudge to harden. It would spin a thread and do other cunning domestic pieces of business, but that was as far as it would go. You might think this would have discouraged me, but hell, I wasn't a great tap-dancer when I started either. As I had gone to Strasberg for acting, so I would go to the greatest authorities on cooking.

The late Dione Lucas, for one. Dione Lucas had a television show, and she was a spectacular cook, but she always made me laugh. Because she said chicking. I'm not making it up. She *did* say chicking. "Take the chicking," she would begin, and I would fall down laughing and miss the next six steps.

Jim Beard was no better. I bought his book because he looked so round and pink and rosy on the cover that I assumed he knew whereof he ate. "Shall I compare me to a fat gourmet?" I would hum, while flipping through Jim Beard's pages, but in the end he made me nervous. He's very opinionated. Rhapsodizes over squabs ("tender and delicious"), for instance, and then doesn't have a good word for ducks. Just tells you how to cook them. An insecure person starts worrying about his taste for ducks. How good can ducks be if Jim Beard doesn't care for them? Also, Jim Beard is a big liar. "The soufflé is simple to make, and not fussy about the way it is baked," Jim Beard says. Take that for gospel and you'll end up talking to your dinner. "Shall I compare thee to a flat soufflé? Thou art more lumpy, and more glutinous. . . ."

Or grutinous, as my Chinese cooking teacher puts it.

My Chinese cooking teacher is a whole other case; I came to her, egged on, as you might say, from common omelets to foo yungs by way of a newspaper item.

A friend who was *not* an actor, and therefore *not* regularly unemployed, sent me the clipping. It said that so many people in New York were eating Chinese food that Chinese restaurants were having a hard time finding chefs. An actor who could cook first-rate Chinese food would not only be able to turn out an unusual résumé ("1970: appeared as the maid in *The Shanghai Gesture;* also furnished forth the baked spareribs and cooked all other props used in banquet scene") but, said my friend, such an actor could earn a good part-time living. And fill his pocket with shrimp rolls to take home.

Charmed, if not entirely convinced, I signed up for Chinese cooking lessons. Me and a bunch of other hopefuls.

The women were a gabby lot, but the tiny Chinese figurine who stood there between the stoves and the sinks and demanded order was more than a match for them.

Her name was Lois Wong, and her little hands, which could chop, slice, dice, stir, roll, seal, pat, were not only capable but incredibly graceful. At rest, the hands curved from the wrists, the fingers shaping themselves into balletic gestures. But what I worshiped about Mrs. Wong was her English.

She didn't just fracture English; she crumbled it, poured soy sauce on it and passed it around for our delectation. First off, she lived on Harry Hassan Parkway in the Bronx. While we were working that out, she described a venerable metropolis in China as an "ain-sint shitty," and extolled the virtues of cartilage in meat. Shin beef got her vote, not only because "the flavor tastier than chuck, but if you cook long, the carteridge still chewy. Carteridge is pro-ting. It's a good stuff."

We heard tales of the various rivers of China, one famous for shrimps which gourmets would travel hundreds of miles to consume. Live. Mrs. Wong's lovely hands sculpted an imaginary basket in the air, plucked an imaginary cover up at one corner; quick as a flash, imaginary chopsticks flew into the basket, flew out again, and the lid clamped down. As the chopsticks were lifted to Mrs. Wong's lips, she described the shrimp she was about to devour. "Still jumping," she said proudly.

Mrs. Wong taught us about Chinese teas—"lichee tea can only flavor, cannot visible, like jasmine"—and Chinese booze, about a rice wine a little heavier than sherry which "has fragrant different to sherry," and a strong pure white liquor called *kao lian,* "like ging, like vogga."

"Most Chinese ladies don't drink," Mrs. Wong said solemnly. "Habit or customer. I different. I drink. Let me confession. I start very early."

She was proud but not surprised about the growing popularity of Chinese cuisine in the United States; even the one-time food editor of *The New York Times* had succumbed to its glories. "Ten, fifteen years ago, Craig Craiborne, he don't like Chinese food, he dislike," she said. "Now after finally getting into it, he don't mind to adjust."

Her skills and her winsomeness had brought Mrs. Wong to the attention of various lecture bureaus, and she often tootled across the country, her cleavers in a small satchel by her side ("Good cook carry creaver with him"), to give demonstrations. Sometimes she and an audience would work at cross-purposes. "I was in Indiana. There was two hunared ladies. So I say, 'Any queshings?' So one lady say, 'Yes, what kinda grasses you wear?' Ooh, I was so mad. I say, 'No queshings about dishes? Only my grasses?' "

She waves her collapsible glasses—a pox on those Indiana ladies—and assures one pupil that MSG won't sicken her ("Don't be afraid, we been using it a thousand years") and another pupil that the lethal-looking cleaver isn't dangerous ("Your right hand will not hurting your left hand with the braid").

She instructs us in how to choose a sea bass—"When the eye is mean and stare at you, that's a fresh fish"—and that onions "should be nice and sweet without mushy," and that "brown rice is a very rough taste" and that a pullet is "a female hasn't made a egg yet. In other words, it's a young lady."

142

She's against our using soap on our woks—"Unless you deep fry a lotta very dirty, no use soap," but she does want us to "ringse well," and she herself ringses rice before cooking because she doesn't like the scum left on unwashed rice after cooking. She shrugs. "So I wash off couple vitamins."

Her measurements (like those of many great cooks) are somewhat haphazard. "Add a little heaping teasponful," she tells us, or "Put a little pork in the block-a-lee." Or "You can also put shredded lettuce. They're very good in fried rice."

Some vegetables are not so easy to decode as block-a-lee. The first time you hear "fresh binker," your mind doesn't leap to offer fresh bean curd, and "cucumbers are horrow" doesn't instantly conjure up the cavity which inhabits the cucumber.

On the other hand, "frank steak" sounds more decent, more honorable to me than flank, and when Mrs. Wong peeled the rind off animal or vegetable, it was for a good reason, namely that she had found "some un-dee-zyble sking."

Ask her a straight question, you got a straight answer. Did she prefer peanut oil or corn oil? "They both I like it." And she was direct about money too. Alarmed over one girl's having dropped out after the first class, she checked her records, looked up and smiled. "It okay, she pay everything," said Mrs. Wong.

We were instructed about bird's nest soup—"This we consider very nutrition"—and the way boys in China climb high cliffs in order to find the special kind of nests that are used. But, said Mrs. Wong, when it came to cooking and eating those nests, "Chinese people very par-tic-oo-lar, got to take the dung and feathers out."

There were wonderful stories about her girlhood in China, and about Chinese festivals, particularly the Chinese New Year.

"New Year's Eve, we burn candles all night long. My mother

143

so stingy with light, but that night, make all through house."

On New Year's Day, relatives would come calling, put money under the kids' "pirrows," and, in most homes, an ancestor table would be set on an altar with a red candle. "Prepare all food to give to ancestor first. But he don't eat, you do."

The Chinese offer food to the kitching god too. "In China, it is very common to place kitching god in kitching, bressing family."

Close your eyes and it's Dione Lucas again, a chicking in every kitching, out-of-work actors behind every wok and pot. Used to be, you could start a fire in the kitchen by rubbing two of my biscuits together; now I can make this airy, fluffy, ethereal dish my teacher so aptly called Crab Meat Crowd.

But will it get me work? In a laundry? As a cook? As a ham?

Or doesn't it matter? What's in a name?

"People," as Mrs. Wong said once, "are very loosely dezzination."

20

The Search for a Best Seller: Valley of the Belly Buttonhole

Chinese cookery isn't the only road open to a starving actor. If you don't want to go around smelling like peanut oil, you can write a dirty book.

This minute, I am sitting here looking at an ad for a book by a lady named Raina Barrett. It is called *First Your Money, Then Your Clothes: My Life and Oh! Calcutta,* and the ad says: "At 31, a suburban housewife, mother, schoolteacher. At 33, living with her lover in Greenwich Village and starring nude on the stage." The publisher describes the author as "an exceptional woman who threw away her ordinary, secure life, to exchange it for the unsure existence of the actress, a sexual life of considerable variety, and a mature understanding that happiness is more than just getting what you think you want. Told with an honesty as compulsive as it is brutal."

Here's to brutal old Raina. It's schoolteachers like her who are going to get our kids back into the classroom.

It used to be when an actress's "sexual life of considerable variety" turned up in print, it was because her husband's lawyer had swiped her diary, and I ought to know because for the past several years, hoping to rip off a best seller if I could find a suitable model, I've been studying the literary output of the theatrical profession. I've memorized books clean and dirty.

145

Not only books by actors, but books by directors. And books *about* actors and directors. And even books about writers who created masterpieces and then the directors stole the credit (Pauline Kael said Orson Welles did Herman Mankiewicz dirty), and books by *other* directors claiming that the *first* directors *deserved* the credit (Peter Bogdanovich said Pauline Kael was crazy). But I have yet to find the volume I can use as a belletristic pattern.

When I first began my search, Billy Redfield had just completed a book about Marlon Brando and Richard Burton. And Richard Burton had just completed a book about Elizabeth Taylor. And Ilka Chase had written a book about the style in which the Russians furnished their visitors' hotel rooms. And Heywood Hale Broun had written a book about how an actor could live off the residuals from television commercials. And Elia Kazan had written a book—his was a novel—about a guy who cheated on his wife.

A *Daily News* columnist named Robert Sylvester said it was strange that Billy Redfield had never "made it big," because he seemed to have more perception about his trade than "the famous and rather dull" stars he was writing about.

That was my dilemma too. I had all this perception, and what I perceived was that none of these tracts was going to serve as my vade mecum to fortune. (Another thing I perceived was that perception was beside the point. Maybe Marlon Brando couldn't "speak the English language"—them were Mr. Sylvester's colors—and for all I knew he couldn't tell time, but he sure could act.)

Briefly I *did* believe that the Burton book about his wife might offer a stealable ground plan. He described Elizabeth at great length. He talked about her stumpy legs, her extra chin, her gray hairs, her praiseworthy bosom.

146

Why, I asked the world, couldn't I describe my husband in a book? The world didn't answer, so I went ahead.

"Michael Chase," I began, "is about six and a half feet tall and always has been. When he was small (as small as anybody six and a half feet tall ever gets) he was also extremely gullible. This gullibility caused him infinite pain. Every day or so, a little bitty kid would come up to him and ask, 'How tall are you?' and Michael would cast his eyes to the ground and try to look humble and say, 'Oh, about six and a half feet tall,' whereupon the little kid would guffaw. 'I didn't know they piled it that high!'

"Michael Chase never caught on. He always bit.

"Michael Chase's feet are permanently fixed at quarter to three, or in first position as we ballet hounds call it. This enables him to walk down a street without being blown over, though a high wind may be tossing others about like autumn leaves.

"When it comes to superb natural endowments, Michael Chase is not far behind Elizabeth Taylor. His Indian name is Many Chins.

"He dresses soberly, in a great gray dirty thing known as 'my director's coat.' It is lined with fleece, and held together at the throat by a simple safety pin. Two of the buttons are missing, and there is no good woman to sew them on, so whenever Michael Chase comes into view, friends and acquaintances greet him alike. 'What the hell kind of a wife have you got?' is the way their greeting goes.

"Michael Chase's socks never matched until his wife threw them out and started over with all black ones.

"Michael Chase can drink more beer than anybody, including Richard Burton, and he can get even sicker.

"He once had a top drawer full of what he called 'neat stuff.' It included stubs of old movie tickets, cellophane bands from cigarette packages (he doesn't smoke cigarettes, he just saves cellophane bands), the ends of shoelaces from which the middles were gone, letters from his mother, keys to a bicycle safely locked in Pittsburgh, and canceled checks without any numbers on them.

"His wife threw out the neat stuff too.

"Michael Chase now has a large Swedish bowl which he refers to as 'my dish' and his new collection of neat stuff reposes therein. It consists of one cuff-link box without cuff links, one chapstick, two three-inch nails, some drapery hooks, a stopwatch, a pocket chess set and a button.

"Sometimes you can hear him talking to himself about his dish. 'Where are my keys?' he will ask, and then answer, 'In my dish,' and he will go and look in his dish and he will find them."

I was finally discouraged from trying to peddle this material by the uncivil suggestion that Michael's not being Elizabeth Taylor (the women's thing is very hot right now) might make a difference when it came to book sales.

The first Kazan novel, *The Arrangement*, was even more out of the question than the Burton work as a blueprint. Though it was printed, and God knows it was blue. The Sunday *Times* reviewer indicated that some parts of it were so out of the question that those parts would also be out of the movie. Private parts. A long soliloquy, for example, in which the hero "addresses his private parts."

Now could I have written a soliloquy addressing Mr. Kazan's private parts? Indeed I could not. They were parts unknown, so far as I was concerned.

Even in those more timid days, I wasn't against tackling *all* daring subjects. A little girl once asked George Abbott if he'd like to hear a dirty word, and while he was trying to look suitably frosty, she cried, "Belly button!" It made me believe that the belly button needed airing.

148

To begin with, the belly button is really a belly buttonhole. Look at it; you'll see I'm right. There was a button there at one time. Mothers of small babies claim to have seen it. But it falls off before a child has reached the age of reason. Or consent. (I put in the sexy stuff to show I could do it if I wanted to.)

Anyhow, once the belly button has fallen off, it leaves the belly buttonhole which we take with us on our later travels.

Why don't people admit this? Why do they persist in euphemism and deception?

The belly buttonhole has been neglected for generations. King Solomon sang about a belly being "as bright ivory overlaid with sapphires." Well, what was holding those sapphires up? I should like to know.

But among the sensation-mongers of the world, belly buttonholes aren't in it with private parts, so that book was never written either.

Perhaps I should have abandoned scruples and got right down to filth. Every family has some dirt in its background, if a commercially minded person were disposed to dig it out. (Dirty underwear. Is there a topic more titillating than underwear? Yet our childhood was one long underwear argument. "Have you got on clean underwear? Suppose you were hit by a car, and you had to be taken to the hospital?" Implicit in the question was the shame of arriving at a hospital maimed, broken and with tattletale gray drawers on. The doctors and the nurses would simply turn away from any child thus attired; they would not even diagnose the case. We all knew that.) But I couldn't hurt my father by washing the family linen in public, so another best seller was consigned to sloshing around in my head.

One of the reasons I continue to have difficulty in deciding exactly which best-seller to write is that the range of literature

149

is so wide nowadays. I get mail from a company which, in order to leaf through its catalogues, you got to be broad-minded. It isn't all about actors, by any means, though there is a "Picture Story of Liz Taylor" book for fifty cents, and one about Clarence Derwent for a dollar. The Derwent one is called "My First Fifty Years in the Theatre" and gives "intimate glimpses and anecdotes of the theatrical great, from the Barrymores to Ginger Rogers." But my catalogue also lists "The ABC of Poultry Raising," "Miss High Heels" ("the extraordinary story of a young Englishman, transformed under the iron hand of his sister into a beautiful young woman!"), "Chinese Self Taught" ("short cuts to learning Chinese, including the 200 best characters") and "Buttock Fetishism," described as "a scholarly study of a bizarre aspect of sexuality. Filled with photographs . . . in the nude or covered by wispy panties."

That's scholarly studies for you. It's no wonder, with the English and the scholars all going to hell in a hand basket, that actors in the 1970s (some of whom do not share my delicatesse) are behaving in an absolutely undignified fashion. David Niven wrote a bawdy book about his early life, Anthony Quinn confessed in a self-portrait called *The Original Sin*, tap-dancer Ann Miller ("she is," said journalist Arthur Bell, "to literary biographies what Simone de Beauvoir is to tap dancing") told about the oil barons and bullfighters who'd chased her to the top, and a kid named Lance Loud, who isn't even a real actor yet (he and his family stood—though not exactly still—for a television documentary called "An American Family," during the course of which director and camera crew came to live with them and shot three hundred hours of film, each and every hour of which now makes the family sick), is forking out into print too. Lance plans to call his autobiography "Leap from the Looking-Glass: The Story of a Teen-Age Whore."

150

Listen, Lance, I'm going to tell you something with an honesty as compulsive as it is brutal. Happiness is more than just getting what you think you want.

Unless what you think you want is a best seller.

21

Watch That Height!

I have had a good many agents. More agents than jobs is one way of looking at it.

My first agency was the Music Corporation of America. Don't it roll off your tongue? Lee Strasberg's wife Paula (who died a few years ago) had written a kind and flattering note about me to the lady at MCA who was then handling the Strasbergs' daughter Susan and who agreed to handle me.

This lady was formidable. She had gray hair and a deep voice, she wore sweaters and pearls and she owned a horse. She had a client list which, even with me on it, she limited to about twelve people—I was the only one I'd never heard of—and she was so busy trying to figure out these famous people's carfare to and from Bangkok, she didn't have much spare time.

Once in a while she would look up from her handicapping sheet—the other thing she did besides figure carfare was figure ponies—and tell me, in her deep voice, "Wear white gloves."

(It wasn't that she wanted me to play admirals, but she had agented for Grace Kelly, and Grace had always worn white gloves; so far as MCA knew, she wore 'em around the brickyard while waiting for her break, and today that simple Philadelphia girl is a major royal.)

I said I saw my agent once in a while, but really, I only went to MCA about twice the whole time I was signed there. Both these times, after I had reintroduced myself, my agent would put down her racing form and tell me to wear white gloves. Then she would revolve me in front of another member of the staff. "Look at that pro-feel," she would say. "Isn't that movie money?"

"Hmm," the person to whom my pro-feel was being extended would reply, while backing toward the door. I suppose ideal beauty is not easy to cope with when it bursts on you unawares; I should of put a white glove over my pro-feel and pulled it off slow, so's they wouldn't get the whole radiance all at once.

MCA never did trade me for movie money (the Kubrick adventure had happened before I came to them), mostly, I expect, because they never could remember who I was. And I didn't dare to call up and bother such an important outfit. Though every day I thought about ways to do it, like dialing the number and saying, "I wonder if Marlon or any of your other biggies would like to know a way to stretch a can of tuna by adding toast crusts and reconstituted lemon rinds," and then, as MCA was getting ready to write down the recipe, sneaking in, "What about me to play *The Three Sisters?* In alpha-bettally order." (A soldier friend bequeathed me that word, learned from a sergeant: "Now all you men get fell in there in alpha-bettally order.")

My news from the world of tuna wouldn't have worked anyway. Nothing worked at MCA. Especially me.

Old joke (in order to understand which you must first understand that MCA had offices in London, Rome, Paris, etc.):

First actor: "Yippee! I just signed with MCA!"

Second actor: "Great. Now you can be unemployed all over the world."

It occurs to me that there may be somebody who doesn't know how a theatrical agent operates. He operates on behalf of the producer is how. That is, a producer calls an agent, says, "I need a girl, eighteen to twenty-six, fat, blue eyes, cockney accent, and she has to wear white gloves." The agent promptly dispatches to the producer six or seven such girls. He is not so much servicing his clients, who must compete against one another, as he is servicing the producer.

All the other agencies in town are also sending fat cockneys to the producer and the lucky girl who gets the part gets to pay her agent 10 percent of her salary.

Actually, MCA was no worse than any other big agency. It was known as the octopus, but its right tentacles seldom guessed what its left tentacles were doing.

Once in a restaurant a guy came over to me and said he was an agent and I had "money bones" and to come see him, and I said where are you? and he said MCA, and I said I'm already your client, and that made him so mad he stalked away.

The Justice Department finally put MCA, which had gradually become a huge packager of television shows, out of the talent business on antitrust grounds. (Not only were they sending every girl on their list for the same job—the Justice Department didn't care about *that*—they were also being the producers to whom they sent every girl, and arguing with themselves about her salary.) A gaggle of FBI men with machine guns came running into those dark wood-paneled offices with the English hunting prints on the walls and caught the malefactors dead to rights with the keys to the men's rooms still unswallowed.

I once invited my horsy lady to see a play off Broadway. I thought she'd want to, not only because the playwright was an MCA client but because I had a fantastic part, and besides, we were closing Sunday night.

"Please come," I said. "It's the last weekend."

"I can't," said my agent.

Silence.

Finally my agent, who lived at the Plaza Hotel, spoke again. "I have to clean my room," she said.

Boy, she was immaculate. She once had me walk with her to Bonwit Teller, where she bought a bar of soap for five dollars. I had never seen anybody buy a five-dollar bar of soap before. Not to use, anyway. To put on the mantel, maybe. I thought it was even classier than those mink-lined raincoats that you can't see the fur when the coat is closed. It's really the reason I stuck with the horsy lady. I was hopeful that part of her soignée would rub off on me, but my father says it was only part of her horse that took.

There always seem to be more male agents than females at the big corporations, but the littler agencies have often been run by ancient women with vague streaks.

The late Mary Welch, who was a big girl, had one of these dippy old ladies nurturing her career. One day as Mary was leaving the office, the old lady called after her. "Dear," she said thoughtfully, "you're getting very tall. Watch that height!"

And I knew another girl who'd already been cast in a new show, and who phoned her representative to see how much money she'd be getting. "I'm calling about *A Thousand and One Nights in Bessarabia*" (or whatever the name of the play was), she said. "Oh, sweetie," said her agent, "there's nothing in that for you. . . ."

My actor friend from Chicago may have had the dippiest-old-lady agent of all. She woke up one morning and fired all her clients. "I had a dream last night," she said. "God came to me and told me to get out of the business."

(The business is what you're in—and also what you get—but long ago it was known as the profession. I worked with a character woman who said that when *she* was a girl, actors could walk

155

into any theatre free by going up to the box office, showing their Equity cards and inquiring, "Do you honor the profession?")

I never had an agent I wasn't scared of, and I had about a dozen of them. The way I went from one to another was a credit to my race. (The sallow race. I'm not exactly white, but I'm not a rich warm brown or a good clear yellow either.) I'd meet a new agent. It would be like a love affair. He or she would tell me how neglected I'd been (true), how nobody understood me (truer), how with him or her guiding me, I'd (1) get to live in that house on the beach that Joan Crawford owned in *Humoresque*, (2) have all the Broadway theatres renamed after me, (3) develop the kiss that conquers and (4) never again be out of work. (False, false, false.)

I believed every single agent. Sequentially. And I was canny in my cowardice. "If *you* will write to my present agent," I would say to each new agent, "and ask for my release, I will sign with you."

Each time, the new agent would write to the old one. Then the new love affair would turn into a marriage. An ill-fated one. You needed too much, they had little to give and felt guilty about it, and after a while they disliked you for making them feel so guilty. They couldn't create jobs, they couldn't make producers and directors want you, and *their* mothers got sick, and *their* rent came due, and you bored them. When they stopped telephoning, it was time to drift away.

I tried all kinds of combinations. Two guys in a phone booth looked good to me for a while because I figured they'd be hungry. So that made three of us. Bad figuring. I went the dippy-old-ladies route; two of them owned the agency and "in a small agency you get individual care." ("Never tell anybody your age," said one. "How old are you?" said the other.) And from them I fled back into the corporate arms of William Morris

156

(after a stop with Ashley Famous, also a conglomerate of many parts, few of them, unfortunately, for me). It must be what you're imprinted with. A bunch of baby geese thought Konrad Lorenz was their mother, and MCA had spoiled me for lunch in Schrafft's.

I enjoyed William Morris because there were so many guys around that if half a dozen of them didn't like you, it didn't matter; *somebody* up there was bound to think you were fine.

At William Morris, a man named Abe Lastfogel was the Big Daddy. Or, rather, the Little Daddy. Mr. Lastfogel, I have always heard (I never clapped an eye on him), is a diminutive gentleman, and there are many jokes about William Morris's hiring only short agents (the rule of Tom Thumb, you might call it; nobody was allowed to be taller than the typewriters with their covers on) so no follower would loom larger than his leader.

Back in the days when producer Walter Wanger shot MCA agent Jennings Lang in the groin (because of Lang's attentions to Wanger's wife, Joan Bennett), ribald conjecture about Wanger's aim circulated coast to coast. "If it had been a William Morris agent, he'd have got his head blown off."

Once, when Mr. Lastfogel had traveled from his California headquarters to New York to clean up some business, he put a secretary to work making phone calls for him.

"Get me Tony Franciosa," he said at one point.

Tony Franciosa is, of course, an actor, but in the New York office of William Morris there labored an agent named Tony Fantozzi (pronounced Fan-toes-zee) and his was the name the secretary thought Mr. Lastfogel had uttered.

So she dialed Tony Fantozzi, and Mr. Lastfogel picked up the phone. "Let's have lunch," he said. "I want to talk about the soandso deal."

Tony Fantozzi was delighted by the boss having singled him out, but after he'd hung up he began to think about it and he realized there must have been an error. He called Mr. Lastfogel back. "Mr. Lastfogel," he said, "this is Tony Fantozzi. I was just talking to you and—"

"Oh, Tony," said Mr. Lastfogel, "I wanted Tony *Franciosa*. . . ."

Tony Fantozzi paused for the space of a heartbeat. Then he said, "Does this mean lunch is off?"

For the past few years, I've had an agent who's a friend. She doesn't know Peter Brook, or Fellini, or Sir Laurence Olivier, or any of the people I'd like to work for, but she does know me. She thinks I'm better-looking than Catherine Deneuve and almost as smart as Lassie. (I have an acquaintance who's jealous of all the work Lassie gets and resents her being so much cleverer than her owners. "They're all sitting down to dinner," he snarls, "and smoke is pouring out the windows, and nobody notices till Lassie jumps up and writes 'Fire' in the mashed potatoes.") Mostly, my agent keeps her thoughts about my brains and beauty to herself, because it might be too painful if outsiders—David Lean, Antonioni, Ingmar Bergman—didn't agree, but I understand.

I think agents are sort of like the ASPCA. When I was a kid, a cat got way up in a tree near our house, and it was clinging, terrified and howling, to a great branch silhouetted against the sky, a branch that looked to us children to be about a mile high. So we called the ASPCA, and the ASPCA couldn't have been nicer. "You put that cat in a box," said the ASPCA, "and we'll be right over."

If you happen to go out on your own and get a job in the theatre, your agent will be right over. And sometimes an agent will come to see you in stock, and send you a telegram opening night, and once in a while an agent will even believe in you.

I've learned from all my agents. I thought my horsy lady was full of it, but since then I've heard that Lynn Fontanne wears *two* pairs of white gloves, one on top of the other (the top ones are slipcovers, torn off in the wings as she glides onstage), and that's good enough for me. Though it's hell while I'm doing this typing.

22

Hope Is the Thing with Horsefeathers

A few seasons back, I traveled off Broadway to see a "showcase" production of three short plays put on by a group in what was surely an abandoned Turkish bath. A mimeographed handout said the actors were being given the chance to work "without commercial pressure." (Translation: The company had liberated its members from the burden of salaries.)

The first playlet featured a large black lady sitting and gazing into a mirror while a small white chap wearing a Castro cap and a Castro beard hopped around on one foot and tried to bite the large lady's ear. All over the stage in front of the couple were strewn newspaper-wrapped bundles daubed with a lurid shade of red paint. Wet, nasty-looking. You knew they held something awful, though you didn't know what. Then the lady wheeled on the guy and chewed him out for having chopped their babies into pieces. With this hint to guide you, you began to be able to distinguish tiny rubber hands and feet sticking out of the newspaper-wrapped packages, as the large lady addressed the small man. "I don't know what's got into you, Al," she said tiredly. "I think you must be going out of your mind."

I'm only telling the story so people who think off Broadway is all Joe Papp and that fancy outfit which produces Edward Albee will appreciate that nature in the theatrical raw is still available to the adventurous.

Traditionally—because there *were* no traditions—off Broadway has provided an atmosphere of freedom: freedom for the actors to go hungry, freedom for the producers to go broke, freedom for the audiences sitting on folding camp chairs to get sharp pains in the behind.

Off Broadway broke down barriers (often was heard an indelicate word, and we saw naked apes of all sexes) to the point where Chekhov-lovers were begging for the pale to be reconstructed, and people who didn't like to be blindfolded when they entered a theatre, or verbally assaulted by raging performers, went so far as to sit around wishing for a revival of *The Drunkard.*

(Which they could also have found off Broadway; in a basement furnished with long wooden tables where patrons may sit and drink beer, a revival of *The Drunkard* has been running for years.)

Off Broadway's innovations—nudity, obscenity and interracial rudeness—are now taken for granted, where once they shocked. I remember my sister's complaining about an off-Broadway show called *Harry, Noon and Night.* She said she couldn't make head or tail of it, though the way she described it, tail was its very essence. "It had a big bed onstage," she said, aggrieved. "And a toilet. And men having sex."

In the seventies that sounds positively stodgy. In the seventies we're told that the producer of one off-Broadway rock musical brought in a doctor to shoot his cast full of speed every night before the curtain went up.

Some off-Broadway theatres are luxurious, rich people's toys fashioned of plush and crystal; some tend more toward exposure, and I don't mean indecent, I mean plaster and water pipe.

My husband's off-Broadway gambols have always sounded more interesting to me than my own, though that may be because he's a good storyteller.

161

Mike once produced and directed a play in a room behind a Greek restaurant, one flight up from the street. There was a guy named Sonny Hayes, who'd started a telephone-answering service for actors, and who'd prospered in this line of work. But Sonny Hayes was no soulless tycoon; when Mike came to him with the idea of a company to be called the Sonny Hayes Circle Theatre, Sonny Hayes came up with fifty dollars. (Early off-Broadway entrepreneurs were so resourceful they could have brought you the chariot race from *Ben Hur* for a hundred bucks.)

The Sonny Hayes Circle Theatre elected to put on an O'Casey one-act. The Greek restaurant owner loaned them his back room because he believed audiences would stop to eat on their way through. And an artist contributed a nonrepresentational set with one pane of real glass stuck into a painted window. This was so an actor could knock a broom through it and break it and hear the audience gasp. Mike procured his windowpane by going into a phone booth, where he found a small piece of glass protecting the message about how to dial long distance. The glass slid out very easily, Mike says.

He recalls the O'Casey as having gone good but not great. Robert Whitehead, a Broadway producer, came to see it—he was a friend of Mike's mother—and said it was interesting.

Mike couldn't take yes for an answer. "If you don't tell me the truth, how can I fix it?"

Whitehead wouldn't budge. Interesting was the word he stuck with.

The people who ate at the Greek restaurant both got sick and held it against Mike.

But Sonny Hayes loved it, Mike says.

Then the Sonny Hayes Circle Theatre moved on to loftier quarters. (Not loftier if you're counting steps; loftier if you're counting closeness to God.) Because the minister of St. Mark's in-the-Bowery offered his church for a production of *Murder in the Cathedral.*

This time Whitehead didn't come, but he sent his casting director. She slept through the whole thing. A CBS casting director came too. He stayed awake, and that was worse. He went back to CBS and imitated the line readings of all the actors, and mocked their hand gestures. (In those days Mike was working at CBS, typing contracts for the casting department and burying, under a piece of carpet, the forms on which he made mistakes. Nobody ever seemed to notice this, which makes you wonder about the CBS casting department. Though some of the other employees made up in efficiency what Mike lacked. When a contract came back from an actor who'd refused to sign a loyalty oath, Mike's friend Joel Herman just signed the actor's name for him and sent the contract on. "I like the guy," Joel Herman said.)

Even Sonny Hayes hated *Murder in the Cathedral.*

But the minister loved it, Mike says.

Then Mike started a repertory company called APA. (Like the Phoenix Theatre, in whose embrace it now rests, APA has itself risen several times from ashes.) "Mike Chase?" you're saying. "Who is Mike Chase? I never heard Mike Chase, the sweetheart of APA, I only heard Ellis Rabb." Well, a wife is here to set the story straight.

Ellis Rabb and Mike had known each other as drama students at Carnegie Tech. After they came—separately—to New York, they would occasionally meet. And Ellis Rabb said he was tired of playing laconic ministers, and Mike said the only way Ellis Rabb was going to get the parts he wanted was to start his own theatre and hire himself. And Mike said he ought to know because nobody was hiring him either.

They incorporated. They went to a lawyer's office on a Saturday afternoon—"so we could use the board room" (off Broadway, you seize your opportunities where and when you find them)—and they birthed the Association of Producing Artists.

Later on, the Association of Producing Artists decamped for Bermuda and Mike, who by then had a wife (not me) and babies, couldn't afford to quit CBS and was left behind.

In every possible way. When APA returned and put on *The Seagull*, they charged Mike to get in. And when they issued an anniversary program listing the name of every director, producer and stagehand who'd ever come near them, his was the only name left off.

He says, belligerently, that he doesn't care. He says he got nervous around most of the people in APA; they were all so piss-elegant they made him want to scratch and talk like John Wayne.

My personal off-Broadway career was brief, but encompassed a wide variety of experience.

First I was in *The Threepenny Opera*. I know you didn't think I could sing. The producers of *The Threepenny Opera* didn't think so either. They fired me, a happenstance which infuriated me at the time but which I now realize saved my liver.

Because I had to get very drunk in order to be a soprano.

In my defense, I ought to say I hadn't yearned for a part in *The Threepenny Opera*. I didn't even know what *The Threepenny Opera* was. I had never heard of Brecht or Weill or Lenya. Unlike Napoleon (who is reported to have said, at the battle of Waterloo, "I wish it were night or the Prussians would come"), I had little interest in the Germans or their arts.

If I had maintained this indifference, I might have been left with my pride. I had been sent down to the Theatre de Lys on Christopher Street because the *Threepenny* people needed a

164

girl to play a baby whore in a bordello scene and, incidentally, to understudy the role of Polly Peachum.

Polly was being sung by Jo Sullivan, a pretty, slender creature, and the main thing her understudy was required to do was fit her costumes.

This became clear at my singing audition. "I don't know why I'm here," I said. "I don't sing opera."

"Sing 'Happy Birthday,'" they said.

I said no.

"Sing 'Three Blind Mice,'" they said.

I said no.

"What do you want to sing?" they said.

I said I didn't *want* to sing anything, but I *would* sing "Why Was I Born?"

Okay, they said, and was I sure the costumes fitted?

Being an understudy is all right. Once. I loved the rackety *Threepenny* orchestra, I grew to love the score (the only person I knew who hated it was Frank Loesser; he used to come down to the theatre to pick up Jo Sullivan, who was his girl, but he'd wait for her in a bar up the block so he wouldn't have to hear the music) and I found backstage an unending carnival.

It was so noisy in the half hour before the curtain went up that the stage manager was forever rushing upstairs to complain that the audience could hear us out in the house; we were louder than the tuning-up sounds of the orchestra. "This is your last warning," the stage manager would say sternly. "I'm not coming up here again."

"Promises, promises," the unrepentant actors would shout after his retreating back.

Jo Sullivan and I shared a dressing room the size of a canary cage, with a piece of sheeting closing it off from a public corridor. All the dressing rooms at the de Lys were like that; Lotte

Lenya, *Threepenny*'s star, widow of its composer, owner, in fact, of the rights to the show, was in the canary cage right next to ours. Backstage at *Threepenny*, I was promptly introduced to the way musical-comedy actors talk. They talk dirty. When they found out I was a prude, they were enchanted. Every night I'd come to work and there would be dirty words and limericks written in lipstick across my mirror, and three or four of my co-workers standing around waiting to see me turn red, sputter and scrub out the graffiti.

Today I talk as bad as anybody, but I look back with a certain amount of affection and regret on that self-righteous girl who wanted to be part of the gang and couldn't find a way to do it.

Jo Sullivan left *Threepenny* to go to Broadway in *The Most Happy Fella,* and I became, ready or not, Polly Peachum. A terrified Polly Peachum. I who couldn't sing in front of my father without turning my face to the wall went forth nightly to offer arias in public. And a pint of brandy went with me, sloshing around in my otherwise empty stomach.

A boy who cared for me used to push me on from the wings, catch me when I came off again, guide me back upstairs and tell me it was okay, but it wasn't okay, it was terrible. And considering that I couldn't read music, or tell a downbeat from a wave on a street corner (when Lenya said I was a mezzo, I thought it was Italian for mess), the miracle is that I lasted until they found another girl who was the right size for the wardrobe.

Highlights and lowlights of my tenure with *Threepenny:*

1. The day I overheard Bea Arthur (television's "Maude"), with whom I had to sing a duet, talking tough about me to one of the producers. "Give her some rehearsal or get rid of her," she was saying. I was crushed, but hindsight suggests that hers was the act of a friend. She didn't enjoy looking bad out there,

166

and she knew it wasn't going to do me any good to look bad either.

2. The night Lenya fell into the bass drum in a blackout. (Subtitled: When they finally picked her up, she was out colder than a mackerel.) Ordinarily, at a certain point in the show there was a blackout, and then the lights would come up and Lenya, followed by a comic named Eddie Lawrence, puffing on a cigar, would cross the stage. This particular night, the blackout occurred and there was a horrendous crash. When the lights came up, there was no Lenya, only Eddie Lawrence plodding across the stage puffing on his cigar. He ambled into the wings and the stage manager grabbed him. "Where's Lenya?" the stage manager cried. Eddie Lawrence flicked a bit of ash from his cigar. "In the pit, I think," he said.

3. The matinee when it was reported that Marlon Brando was out front. He didn't come back and say I was good. On the other hand, he didn't come back and say I wasn't good. I rest my case. It was a case of brandy anyway.

My next off-Broadway employment was as a golden-haired princess in a pseudo-Greek drama. All the characters were kings and messengers with unpronounceable names, and I quit a week before we were to open because I'd been offered the lead in an off-Broadway revival of a play called *Mrs. Patterson*.

Taken all in all, I felt more about *Mrs. Patterson* than I have about any other theatre experience. It offered one of the best parts ever written for a girl (she could make the audience laugh in the second act and weep in the third) and though we did it in the late fifties, I was convinced then that everything afterward would be downhill.

The play told the story of a Southern waif whose mother

worked as a maid. In the original production, the little girl and her mother had been black (Eartha Kitt starred on Broadway), but few line changes were necessary because the script isn't about color, it's about starvation, about a kid starved for food that isn't handouts, for clothes that aren't castoffs, for love, which she believes has run off to Chicago in the person of her father.

Mrs. Patterson was written by a black playwright named Charles Sebree. A firefly of a man, he blazed and went out while you looked at him, his brilliance vitiated by his insecurities. In encounters with the white world, he was guarded, vulnerable; he could not sustain his confidence long enough to protect his work from marauders.

Slender, with a narrow mustache and a soft voice, Sebree walked so lightly you couldn't be sure he had a shadow, and he would sit in a corner at rehearsals never saying a word. During the entire rehearsal period, I only heard him speak once. It was on a day when I blew up at the director and stalked toward Charlie's corner. He looked up at me and grinned. "You got to cool it, baby," he said.

He cooled it too much, never fighting for himself, though he had done battle on my behalf, a fact I only found out later. (At my first reading, after I'd finished a long speech, Charles had spoken into the silence. "I never heard the words before," he said. And though the director told him privately that he still wanted to see other girls, Charles had prevailed.)

His original script had been called *Late Dry August*—"It took me eight years to write it, sittin' behind a coal stove in a basement"—and the Broadway managers who'd put it on had called in a play doctor–coauthor who'd added whimsy and a couple of fantasy sequences. But I believe in my bones that the grit of the play was Charlie's, and the ache.

168

There was a scene in which the mother (whom the child holds in contempt for accepting the crumbs off a rich lady's table) talks about sitting on the broken front porch in the twilight, imagining she sees her long-gone husband coming up the road, only to have what she sees turn out to be a shadow.

During the last act, the child, whose plan to escape up North on a freight train has been thwarted, and whose bravado has been pierced by the realization that her mother is lonely, too, turns to the woman. "You ain't no shadow on the road, Mama," she says. "You always come home."

I was never able to finish the line. I would reach out, touch the hair of the actress playing my mother, and choke halfway through the words.

All through the rehearsal period, Sebree and I would confer by telephone in the middle of the nights, because he was too shy to challenge mistakes made at the theatre and we knew there were problems to solve. There was a strange identification between us; it was as though I had turned into the kid he had written, the kid he used to be.

After we opened, I couldn't shake the play even when I was away from it. I cried at home, I cried at the theatre, I didn't want to see anybody or talk to anybody or eat my breakfast or know about the world outside *Mrs. Patterson*. Sebree laughed and said Eartha Kitt had been affected the same way. "Her maid used to say, 'Charles, you got to do somethin' about Eartha, she's cryin' again.'"

Mrs. Patterson opened in a famous off-Broadway theatre called the Davenport, and though the brownstone is still there —in the East Twenties, near Lexington Avenue—it has another name now, which is, I think, too bad.

According to theatrical folklore, the place had once been known as the Davenport *Free* Theatre. An old actor named

Davenport had lived and worked in it. Audiences didn't have to buy tickets; they would just come in and sit down, and Mr. Davenport would wail away at soliloquies from *Hamlet* and *Lear* and later on pass a hat.

Mr. Davenport was still alive, renting out his theatre and living up top somewhere, while we were doing *Mrs. Patterson*. The parlor floor, where the audience could circulate during intermissions, was lined with framed pictures of stage performers of another age, and the auditorium itself, always too steamy or too cold, was full of ghosts.

Sometimes, during rehearsals, you'd glance up suddenly and catch a glimpse of a black-clad figure standing at the back of the little balcony, a cape slung from his shoulders, looking like the Phantom of the Opera, or *Don Giovanni*'s statue of the Commendatore, come to life.

He could no longer operate in the world which had pushed so harshly through his doors; for him it was too late, and for Sebree it may have been too early.

If Sebree had come along now, when there's a ferment of black theatre and black pride, would he have stayed with it? Would he have got the attention he deserved? Or am I romanticizing? Maybe he didn't really care about being a great American playwright. Certainly he was a dilettante—he'd tried all kinds of lives, quitting the Village because "I was tired of sitting around on the floor, drinking that Chianti wine," leaving the Katherine Dunham troupe, in which he'd been a dancer, abandoning tennis, though he played well enough to teach, not even concentrating on his painting though he was a painter whose canvases were valued (producer Leonard Sillman collected Sebrees)—and certainly he was a kind of genius. Often I wonder where he got to, and what he did there.

The last time we met, he borrowed twenty dollars. I hated to let him have it because I knew it meant I would not see him again.

It's possible, of course, that what Sebree and I had shared was nothing more special than hope. If "hope is the thing with feathers," off Broadway should look like a mile and a half of Lillian Russell's hats. Off Broadway, everybody lives on hope. Everybody. In their houses which seat 299 people (more than 300, and they're dealing with uptown union rates), the producers hope. Though it isn't easy to meet your nut, let alone turn a profit, with a 299-seat house. And the actors hope. An actor will give up his weekly unemployment check to take an off-Broadway job at less money. And he will embark on those killing weekends (off Broadway runs on a queer schedule: you play five of your eight weekly shows between Friday night and Sunday night), hoping against hope that somebody besides his mother will show up to see him.

Money is never the issue, because if what you really want is money, you don't go into the theatre. Off Broadway, people are hoping to use themselves; designers, actors, writers, all of them so longing to work that they go ahead under improbable conditions; desperate for action, they fly in the face of realities.

And while, from a businessman's point of view, that may be a mistake, it's a very interesting mistake. Because off Broadway may be the only place where someone will let an actor play Shakespeare or Ibsen, or he'll get the chance to help a new writer test himself. And that's what being an actor is about, residuals for commercials and bit parts on "Mannix" notwithstanding.

For a person who studies acting and dreams of doing the great roles, it's probably more sensible to hang around off Broadway than to hang around Los Angeles, hustling for enough series shots to pay the rent.

171

Out there, hope dies too cruelly; off Broadway, it doesn't even have sense enough to know it's sick.

A friend of mine was acquainted with a fledgling playwright who'd managed to get his opus put on in an off-Broadway playhouse. The reviewers savaged it. The second night, my friend went down to the theatre. There were four people in the audience, but the author said he was going to keep the show running. Out of his own pocket.

Three days later, my friend went back again. This time there were six people, and he knew four of them were in on passes.

He hurried backstage to see the author. "How are you?" he said.

"Very encouraged," said the author. "It's building."

That's hope. And that's off Broadway.

23

Broadway: A wide open road or highway, as opposed to a narrow lane or byway

(Oxford English Dictionary)

I almost forgot the best hope I ever heard. Once, on an opening night, in the midst of great flurry, I met a character man who seemed more than usually discomfited, and for some reason I took it into my head that he was searching for something I could supply.

"Do you have enough makeup?" I asked him.

He looked at me kindly. "I hope I live as long as I've got makeup for," he said.

Next to wanting to live, most actors want to play on Broadway. Or they used to. Nowadays, in certain circles there's an equal and opposite reaction against Broadway, the reverse snobbery of those who, having been unwanted, no longer want. Experimental theatre groups, classical theatre groups, regional theatre groups—many of these scorn what Broadway has to offer and consign its overstuffed, boorish expense-account audiences to darkness and David Merrick. (Who's glad to get them.)

But if you grew up at the movies (television babies are fed different stuff), an aspiring actress was offered a blueprint for her future.

With the dangers laid out. There were movies about girls who

173

turned their backs on sweeping and motherhood and their own true loves in order to climb the Broadway heights, and these girls often ended up alone, taking in washing or drinking. (Not taking in drinking, dummy.)

For every light on Broadway there is a broken heart.

And then there were movies about ambitious actresses pandering to the lusts of powerful, sadistic men in order to achieve Broadway stardom, and these men would use these actresses and cast them aside like burned-out bulbs.

For every heart on Broadway, there is a broken light.

In movies, a heroine almost always gained theatrical prominence at the expense of a Broadway star. The Broadway star was vulnerable to a special set of dangers. A star might die at sea, and the heroine replace her. Or a star might fight with her producer and quit the show, and the heroine might replace her. Or a playwright (young), director (sensitive) or producer (with crisp curls) might fall in love with the heroine and fire the star, etc.

It was taken for granted that Broadway stars were fragile, self-indulgent and talentless. (Joke enjoyed by student actors: A performer goes to a psychoanalyst and wails, "Oh, doctor, I'm so unhappy. I can't sing, I can't dance, I can't act." The doctor nods. "Well, why don't you get out of show business?" "I can't," says the performer. "I'm a star.")

But stars, real or fictional, talentless or gifted, have always had one thing in common—the guts to get out there and shine. Humility has no place in the theatre, and to pass the hours hanging around the unemployment office, I have been compiling a list—from information gleaned in the pages of *The New York Times*—of people who could never have functioned on Broadway because they are too humble. These people don't want their names spelled out in lights; they want them writ on

174

water. The first three shrinkers on my list are:

Philippe de Gaulle, son of the late great Charles. Philippe must have been an enigma to his dad. When reporters asked the younger de Gaulle whether he might follow Pops into politics, Philippe said *Non*. "To enter politics, it is necessary to have a personality, and favorable circumstances, and I have neither."

Dikran A. Sarrafian, the Lebanese dealer in antiquities who was involved in the selling of the Euphronios vase to the Metropolitan Museum. He told correspondent Nicholas Gage, "There is nothing about me worth perpetuating. I wasted my life with whores and archeologists."

Eisaku Sato, long-time premier of Japan. Sato may or may not be modest, but his wife is so modest on his behalf that he qualifies. Mrs. Sato confided to the world that Mr. Sato is "not an interesting man, so modern girls never want to marry him."

Lack of personality or favorable circumstances, or a wasted life, or not being interesting doesn't hold a genuine actor back.

The way Hollywood used to tell it, all you had to do was get a bit part, and in short order you would surely replace a star, but real life is chancier.

In my first Broadway show, I replaced a girl who'd been fired. Not only wasn't she the star; she didn't have any lines. To this day, I can't fathom why they let her go. All she had to do was sit onstage and suck a lollipop.

The play was based on a Eudora Welty story called *The Ponder Heart*, and David Wayne was the hero. To impersonate the barefoot, pigtailed, candy-licking kid sister of the ingenue, I was offered eighty-five dollars a week. I think it was eighty-five dollars; it was the Broadway minimum. I believed I should hold out for more. "Well," said Terry Fay, the casting director, "the company manager will be coming around to see you, and maybe he'll have a hundred-dollar gleam in his eye."

He didn't have. I read the message plain in his pupils. Eighty-five bucks and you're lucky to get it.

Since I didn't know why the girl who'd been fired had been fired (Had she walked through the play? There are no small parts, only small actors), I addressed myself to making the most of my time onstage.

My first night in the show, during a courtroom scene (my only scene), I sat on a bench and wriggled and grinned and gasped at the testimony and waved to the jury (I assumed this small-town girl would know everyone on the jury) and acted up a storm. Afterward, Juanita Hall sent me a message by way of the stage manager. When the stage manager told me why he'd searched me out, I grew excited, expecting a compliment for my efforts.

The stage manager dashed this expectation. He maintained that Miss Hall had said, "Tell that brat to sit still."

(I learned several things from Juanita Hall, who was as just as she was candid. The night I went on for a girl—with lines—who was out sick, Juanita was the first person to come and tell me I'd been fine, though she'd had to haul her considerable bulk up five flights of stairs—from where she dressed to where I dressed —to say so.)

The Ponder Heart housed an exotic collection of actors. If you wanted to see the world, getting to know *The Ponder Heart* cast was better than joining the navy.

Once Juanita took a box at a fete in one of the big Harlem ballrooms and invited all of us and there was soul food and fantastic entertainment and music.

Once featured player Will Geer gave himself a birthday party in a loft in Chelsea, and the lady on whom Auntie Mame was said to have been based wouldn't serve a piece of birthday cake to anybody whose astrological sign didn't grab her just right,

and of maybe forty guests, thirty had brought guitars, and Will's
ex-wife, a new baby strung papoose fashion from her shoulders,
got up and strummed and sang a greeting.

> Happy, happy birthday, Bill,
> Hip, hip, hip, hooray—
> We hope you plant your garden
> In the usual kind of way

was how it went, and why that burned itself on my brain I
wouldn't be knowing.

And once Yolande Betbeze, a former Miss America, and a
buddy of some of the Southerners in the cast (she was married
to Matthew Fox, then the head of Universal Pictures), enter-
tained us in her penthouse on top of the Universal Pictures
building on Park Avenue, and that *was* just like a movie. I think
Yolande had a butler; I know she had a round bed.

And once one of the character actors asked me to have dinner
with him between matinee and evening shows, and I didn't
want to wound him so I said yes, and instead of leading me to
a coffee shop, he hurtled both of us into the IRT, pushing old
ladies out of our way—it was rush hour—and when we got to
his West Side brownstone walk-up, he sat me in a chair and
played Indian sitar music to soothe his nerves, and he fed me
two scallions, a piece of cheese, a cracker and half a glass of milk
which he'd been storing on a windowsill, and he read me letters
from his mother, and he cried.

After a couple of hours, I cried too.

One thing about Broadway that's interesting: No matter how
truly an actor knows that most of the shows he gets into will
close out of town, or a few days after they come into town, no
matter how weary he gets of living on rehearsal pay, he continues to believe in the big break. Actors are gamblers subsidizing

the horse race which is theatre. One show folds, another is scratched, but the actor keeps pressing, persuaded he must get a winner one day.

The very first Broadway production I ever came in contact with may serve to illustrate the absolute randomness of what can happen to a beginner.

William Inge had written a play called *Bus Stop*. The management wanted Kim Stanley for the lead. Kim Stanley didn't want to play the lead. The management kept making her offers she couldn't refuse. She refused them. So the management began reading other actresses.

They had decided if they couldn't get Kim Stanley, they would go in another direction (that's a big theatrical phrase), look at waifs and strays, since they wanted Cherie, the heroine, to appear to be a teen-ager. A friend from Strasberg's class took me up to the Robert Whitehead office, where I was asked about my stage experience (I hadn't yet had any) and I was introduced to the director, Harold Clurman. He said I could come to the theatre and read.

Already this is unusual. Mostly, inexperienced strivers after glory can't lurch in to see Harold Clurman; he has to be protected from them or he couldn't find time to do his directing. But that day I got lucky.

At the theatre, I got luckier still. The other waifs and strays had been reading Cherie with sympathy for her tough childhood and hard past. I elected to read her like a hillbilly baseball player, half disbelieving, half laughing about what she'd been through.

It worked. They all got up out of their seats in the dark house—Mr. Inge, Mr. Clurman, Mr. Whitehead—and came down to the foots and studied me. They told me to come back tomorrow. They gave me a script to take home.

178

For the next few days, I read with various boys they were considering for the hero. Between readings they kept me in the cellar of the theatre, and an assistant stage manager who was down there, too, and who seemed to have inside information, told me I must be a good girl when we went out on the road.

I was willing to be the best girl he'd ever seen; I only hoped his information was correct. My first Broadway reading, and a part. Not just a part—a huge star part.

P.S. A huge star, namely Kim Stanley, finally decided to do *Bus Stop*. Bad as I felt, I wasn't destroyed, because Kim Stanley was my idol, and losing out to a genius is no disgrace.

P.P.S. They didn't even offer me the understudy. When they don't need you, they don't need you. And what's more, the next time they see you they won't know who you are.

But the excitement of coming that close, and the knowledge that an unknown *can* come that close, helps keep you going.

In the movie *Expresso Bongo* Wolf Mankowitz wrote a line about the theatre. "All you need," he said, "is one good break —after another."

A break at the wrong time is no help either. Frank Loesser once hired another girl for a musical. This was after my friend Jo Sullivan had introduced me to Frank, who was her husband, and he'd liked me, and we'd worked on some of the show's music, and I'd auditioned a good many times, so I was unhappy when I didn't get to play the ingenue. Frank said I should take a job as the ingenue's standby, keep my mouth shut, and wait. He said there were complicated reasons for what had happened in the casting, and he personally didn't think the other girl was going to cut it, and then I'd be right there. I got high church, and said I didn't want a job where I'd have to go to work every night and hope some poor girl would destroy herself, thank you very much, but if you get rid of her,

179

I'll be glad to step in like Judy Garland did in her early pictures.

Then I went to Philadelphia with a different musical. The night the call came, there were fourteen people sitting on the floor in my hotel room, eating sandwiches and drinking beer, and moaning. Actors like to moan. The phone rang and a boy sitting next to it picked it up, looked stunned and announced loudly, "It's Frank Loesser."

A hush fell over the group. I took the phone. On the other end, Frank said, "Don't tell anyone I called. . . ."

He'd fired the ingenue, he needed a new one right away—tomorrow, for instance. Only I'd been so despondent about my life and hard times, I'd spent the last week kissing a chorus boy who had a cold, and I not only couldn't sing, I couldn't croak.

To add to my misery, the show in which typhoid Louie of the chorus and I were stuck was a disaster. It told the story of a girl who worked in a health food store and a man who ran a hippie nightclub. Philadelphia audiences, when they came at all, didn't stay long; they began leaving during the first act, and the actors wished they could go with them. The director quit. An actor took over. No good. Another actor took over. No better. I think the guy from the box office came and put in his two cents' worth (two cents was about what he'd taken in).

Even so, the producers brought that show in to New York. Shut down out of town, and you've lost all the bananas. Turn up at the Martin Beck as though you thought you had something, and maybe New Yorkers will instruct those Philadelphia hicks in the matter of what taste is. *Oklahoma* is fabled for opening badly out of town.

No need to beat a dead horse. The health food musical wasn't another *Oklahoma*.

I did appear in one Broadway musical that lasted through the

180

night—and even a few months longer. It was a George Abbott–directed opus called *Tenderloin*. (Auditioning for George Abbott is practically painless because he makes up his mind in a trice. Halfway through your first song he'll stop you, say thanks, and if he's decided you're what he wants, by the time you've got home and opened your front door, the phone is ringing with an offer.)

In *Tenderloin*, I got to dance a polka with Maurice Evans in what looked like his union suit, but was actually a gay-nineties-style bathing garment.

I also got billing. (Billing means your name appears in the ads.) I was eighth featured player. (Eighth featured billing means seven other actors' names come before yours.)

In New Haven, I lost my voice.

In Boston, I lost my big number. (Though I'd got a review that said I was "the surprise of the evening," and the movies of my childhood had led me to believe such a review would lead to immortality and the firing of the star.)

And Cecil Beaton, who was the designer, studied me with loathing from under his Sherlock Holmes hat and said, "You ah faaah too thin and faaah too pale."

And the actress who was my dressing-room mate, announced darkly that there were too many featured players in the show and I knew she thought one of us should go and it wasn't her she had in mind.

I met Jerome Weidman, who'd written the book for the show, on the street, and he said he never wanted to see Boston again. He'd lost some things too.

By the time we opened in New York, I had more costumes than lines—"There can't be any emphasis on the heroine's girl friend"—and in my humiliation I wanted to quit. I was talked out of this action by Bobby Griffith, a producer whose

181

generosity could make a crow believe it was a nightingale and an actress believe she was irreplaceable.

At the 46th Street Theatre, where we settled for the New York run, I dressed with a woman named Christine Norden and a woman named Marguerite Shaw, and Christine Norden's dog. Christine and Marguerite read feelingly to one another, out of dog magazines, poems that went something like:

> When things begin to ache ya
> And it's rainin', like as not,
> Who will ne'er forsake you?
> Why, your ole dog Spot.

I think I know now where the word "doggerel" comes from.

Once Marguerite started, "Dog spelled backward—" but the shock of recognition hit Christine so hard she howled, and the reading couldn't continue.

Gossip rages backstage (Did the boy singer *mean* to put a Valentine in the boy dancer's mailbox? No, the singer intended the card for Christine. Then the dancer must think the singer's crazy. "Hell no," says the singer. "He thinks I love him") and so do half-baked intellectual discussions about the theatre (Marguerite listened to ours with tolerance: "I don't mind," she said. "I'd just as soon they do plays on psychology or patriotism or all those themes they get") and so do passions.

My passion on Forty-sixth Street was reserved for a small, wiry woman known as Rosie, who was my dresser. She hooked me up, she washed my tights, she brought me gefüllte fish, she ran up and down stairs a dozen times a night cheerfully doing errands for anyone who asked her. Rosie was a widow who'd been married for twenty-five years, and she laughed every time she talked about her husband. "People think I'm crazy, but I remember so many good things."

182

You couldn't tip her—she screwed up her face and snarled if you tried—and her gaiety was tonic. All the little kids in *Gypsy* used to line up to kiss her, and her own children sounded like gag writers.

"She's so neat," complained her son Joel, "that if I get up in the middle of the night to get a drink of water, when I come back my bed's made."

(Not everyone hits it lucky with a dresser. A friend of mine was attended by a lady who had the habit of telephoning at 4 A.M. The drunken dresser would deliver a harangue, then ring off, but not before admonishing my friend. "An' one more thing," she would say. "Please don' call me again a' this hour of the night.")

There is a life which goes on backstage—in any theatre—that's funny and sad and thrilling and tedious all at the same time. You spend so many of your waking hours there, sitting on broken chairs that tear your stockings, among pots of colored paints and dirty towels, and bathrobes with Pancake #4 N stains around the collars, and you're always losing one of your lashes five minutes before the curtain, and the little girl cousins of friends drop by asking to try on "the red-and-white one," and you haul in containers of cardboard-flavored coffee and your lunch on matinee days, and sometimes on a birthday or a holiday or a closing night you share champagne out of paper cups.

There are weeks when it's so cold in your dressing room that you have to board up the windows and complain to Equity, followed by weeks when the heat comes on so strong that you have to tear the boards down and complain to Equity.

And strangers off the street come in to visit you. Even stars aren't proof against a truly determined caller. Maurice Evans once barricaded his dressing room door against a fierce lady who went right on pounding. "Let me in!" she cried. "I have a right to know you; you've been spitting at me across the footlights for twenty years."

Some actors crave to be in a Broadway musical because their hearts crack at the sound of an overture, or because the heat of a follow-spot warms them more than the sun could do, or because they want to grow up to be Bob Fosse, or because they've been locked into Strindberg, and they're wistful, lured by visions of gaudy nights, and the chance to display legs and lungs.

Other performers—who've been successful in musicals—crave to be cast in dramatic parts in straight plays because they believe that's the only way to earn the deepest respect of the profession. Mrs. Siddons wasn't known for her dancing.

But most actors don't care whether it's words or music, just so the beat goes on. There was an adorable old gentleman named Roy Fant playing a bit in *Tenderloin,* and I so admired him that I asked why he'd been willing to take such a minor role.

He shrugged off my fatuity and winked. "It's better than sittin' on my ass over there in the Lambs Club," he said.

24

"The Best Man Amongst Them Durst Not Touch Her Tail"
("Four and Twenty Tailors," Anonymous)

This is my Hollywood chapter because it is no good to write an actor's book without a Hollywood chapter. Even you never went there. Which is not my case; I been.

My fires were lighted when I saw *The Goddess,* starring Kim Stanley. I cried like a baby, during and after.

The Goddess was a movie Paddy Chayefsky wrote about a girl from a small town who goes to Hollywood and becomes a star and sucks up to tycoons and dumps her loving husband and drinks and dopes and dies untimely.

Well, we came out of Loews Sheridan on a Sunday afternoon, my boyfriend of the moment and I, and I cried clear across Washington Square Park and through dinner and halfway into the Ed Sullivan show.

Why not. I knew that was me up there, a comet whose talent would be co-opted by shoddy hucksters; whose beauty, though it caused men to cluster to her ("like mutts around a phlegm," as Marlene Dietrich sings it), would burn out in a blaze of hard sauce and betrayal.

My boyfriend said I didn't have to be a Hollywood star if I felt so bad about it. He said Paddy Chayefsky might not even have the final word on The Way It Is Out There.

But I didn't listen. A comet got no ears. We run more to tail. (In the 1950s there was a bespectacled child star who was a true comet, not only because of his meteoric rise, but also because of his shape. I once heard an out-of-work actress jealously assessing the little chap. "Lookit 'im," she said. "All ass and no eyes.")

Anyway, I sat around on what us comets largely feature, planning my decline into a sick, degenerate movie star, which is the only real kind. (I don't count the Kubrick experience as true movie stardom, and this is for several reasons. One: *He* don't count it. Two: It happened mostly underground—in the Lessinton Ah-venue So-way, as my friend Carmen calls it. Three: There was no makeup man or hairdresser.)

If you inquire don't I know that some people can't be tempted by Hollywood's dirty money and rotten offers, I have to say yes. I admire those people. There's the Spanish director Luis Buñuel. He's so pure that when they asked him if he would go to Hollywood to pick up the Oscar he'd won for *The Discreet Charm of the Bourgeoisie*, he said, "I will never go to that place for any reason." (The purity of Spanish cinema may be endemic. I read in a film catalogue about a Spanish movie called *Where Are You Going, Alfonso the Twelfth?* No peccable Anglo could write that.)

(In)corruptibility where Hollywood is concerned has always come in grades, like motor oil. There's the heavy, or Buñuel, kind. There's the "Tempt me, oh, I hope I'll say no" kind. There's the "I'll just go for a while and save the money and give it to the American Indians" kind. After these, you run into your straight "Smirch me, smirch me, I want a chalet in Switzerland" classification.

Experts will argue that there is no Hollywood anymore, that movies are made the world over, the star system is finished, all you need now is to be a good actor. Tell it to Sweeney, as my grandma used to say. And while you're at it, tell it to Ali Mac-Graw. Maybe she didn't have a forehead (who knew what was under those pot hats?) but she had the boss of Paramount Pictures.

Looking at it one way, a comet bound for Hollywood can't have too much tail, as pieces of it are reputed to get busted off during the heavenly body's rise. Scientifically speaking, this chippage may be due to the weight of salt carried by the appendage. The novelist and poet Samuel Butler was first to suggest this when he said:

> Such great achievements cannot fail
> To cast salt on a woman's tail.

Still, any actress worth her salt is drawn to Hollywood because in Hollywood people continue to have panache. If you don't believe me, read *Women's Wear Daily*. Time and again, *Women's Wear Daily* documents how much more exotic the folks are in the mysterious West. *Women's Wear* will interview a French lady who's working in California and describe the scene thus: "Flashing the huge pink diamond on her middle finger, Renée points out the 190-year-old Venetian dining room chairs and her grandfather's oak coffin which she's transformed into a table accessory for her Century City apartment."

God knows what she's done with her grandfather.

But would you have thought of it? Would I?

I am by now convinced that this lack of imagination is what kept me from running away with Robert Redford (Robert Redford was the other thing that kept me from running away with him) and becoming a superstar.

Because I can't go on lying to you. I'm not really rich, just comfortable. And I'm not really distinguée, just terribly loved and respected.

It might have gone another way, if I'd been willing to dig up Grandpa. Or if I could have stopped eating. It isn't that I didn't go to California a couple of times, but the food out there makes me crazy. I can't think about auditions; I'm too busy stuffing my face with avocados, and sneaking into abandoned gardens and fetching out lemons as big as footballs, and traveling up north for cracked crab (during whatever month that is when the crabs are running or scuttling or cracking themselves), and traveling down south to where the enchiladas are nesting. Even the air in California can unhinge an Easterner. After dark, you can run along the raggedy beaches howling like a dog, so drunk with night stars you forget you've come west on the important business of seducing movie magnates.

Another mistake I made which led to total lack of seduction of movie magnates was I didn't go where they hung out. I think it's Palm Springs, but I never had the cab fare.

Throughout my brief Southern California sojourns, I stayed in an old folks' home that thought it was a *pensione*. It had been recommended by a lady who feared being raped by a bellboy. The *pensione* didn't have a bellboy. It had a couple of hundred-year-old desk clerks (luckily we were only a kidney stone's throw from the Beverly Hills Medical Center) and their ancient glittering eyes were anything but gay. No hope of rape there; hardly any hope of hot water.

And I rode the buses along palm-lined, empty streets, me and a smattering of maids. Some of them may have been magnates' maids, but that never struck me until this minute.

And once I went to meet a famous agent (very patient, very kind), but I already had my ticket back to New York, and when the famous agent asked when I was leaving, I said tomorrow. He said Greta Garbo wasn't made in a day, but I left anyway. I hadn't seen a freak exposing himself in a subway in about a week and a half, and a New Yorker gets homesick.

Maybe the agent couldn't have done anything with me even if I'd stayed. I haven't been sufficiently strict about my art. And I've always got a run in my stocking. I didn't know I wasn't sufficiently strict until I saw a newspaper story about a girl named Marilyn Chambers, who starred in a pornographic movie called *Behind the Green Door.*

For one scene, said the newspaper report, Miss Chambers had performed "simultaneous sex acts with four athletes suspended from a trapeze."

That oughta get the old blood moving. And it was real sex, no faking. Marilyn Chambers said she thought simulated sex was "very dishonest." She also said, "I'm not interested in just screwing in the movies. I'm a serious actress." She said when her day's shooting was over, she went home and washed the dishes "like any other wife."

That girl is practically as pure as a Spaniard.

But I suppose I've been beating around the bush for long enough; it's time for me to admit I never worked in Hollywood. I would admit it like a shot, except I hate for people to say, "What the hell kind of movie star is *that?*" and hurt my feelings, so I'm going to equivocate a little further.

I've worked *near* Hollywood. I played in a big tent outside San Francisco. Does that count? Wait, I can come closer. How about that big tent right across the street from Disneyland?

And I've worked with movie stars. And I've lived in a movie star's garage. And the movie star's wife let me pet the dog.

Ah, it still doesn't come out like *The Goddess.*

A few weeks ago, I was reading a book review and the headline said: "Serious Problem Trivialized." Now I'm sick that if I ever finish committing my life to paper (even the leeriest liver winds somewhere up a tree) and it gets reviewed, the critic is

189

going to say: "Trivial Problem Serialized. Dopey Person Tells of Dopey Adventures."

Can it be that I started too late? Work on one's immortality begins young. I saw a class of third-graders on a television news show, and they had already starred themselves in a couple of movies, and they were only nine years old. They had finished making a horror picture, and were working on a Sherlock Holmes story, when the television reporter took a pigtailed little girl aside and asked her to describe her function.

"I got three jobs," the little girl said. "Dee-rector, cameraman, and I play Professor Muh-mar-ity."

"Moriarty?" asked the reporter.

Pigtails and eyes dancing, the little girl said yes.

Well, which job was hardest, the reporter wanted to know.

"Dee-rector," she said. " 'Cause you always got to be there. And sometime they don't listen."

They certainly don't. None of the bastards listens. If I'd known that much when I was nine years old, I'd have been properly burned out today.

25

More About Broadway: All That Goes Up Must Come Down

No matter how much they admire purity, or commitment to a life in art, most actors have sneaky fantasies about success on Broadway, which is more a place in actors' heads than a confederation of streets and theatres. And because it's part of the same little kid's dream, most actors also fantasize about working with a legendary director; they wonder if his magic is transferable.

It's the same wonder William Butler Yeats expressed about Leda, after she'd taken instruction from a Swan:

> Being so caught up
> So mastered by the brute blood of the air,
> Did she put on his knowledge with his power
> Before the indifferent beak could let her drop?

Yeah, did she? If an actor is caught up by a master builder of the theatre, does the mastery rub off? If he comes under the spell of someone who has accomplished in reality—elegantly and easily—what the actor has only accomplished in his imagination, may the apprentice become a sorcerer?

I don't know, though I was Preston Sturges's last protégé.

The way it happened was a fluke. (Being the sum of my parts, luck, good *and* bad, is what I believe in. It's a magic-think I've heard psychoanalysts deplore, but it does not seem amenable to correction.)

In January of 1959, I was not expecting to meet Preston Sturges. All I knew about him was that he had been a great Hollywood tycoon. Anybody who'd ever read a movie magazine knew that. Later I learned more. In his heyday Sturges had been a major force at Paramount Pictures, he'd built a restaurant called The Players and lost a fortune on it (he'd run both set and restaurant like fiefdoms), he'd hired unknowns and starred them in pictures he'd written, produced and directed.

Today his satires—*The Great McGinty* spoofed politics (Brian Donlevy played a hack who rose to glory), *The Miracle of Morgan's Creek* kidded motherhood (Betty Hutton had a bunch of babies and couldn't remember who their father was), *Sullivan's Travels, The Lady Eve*—are called classics, but somehow I'd never seen one, and by the end of the 50's, Sturges was no longer a name to conjure with. There were stories that he'd been broke and broken when he left Hollywood, and that some there had been glad of it because he'd been arrogant in the days of his power.

And he'd had the power. (Raconteur-painter-writer Alex King once went to several Hollywood morticians and asked whom they'd bury for nothing—just for the publicity—and Louis B. Mayer and Sturges were the two names on every list.)

In the late fifties Sturges was living in France—he'd made a picture there called *The French They Are a Funny Race*—with a young wife (she was thirty-two years his junior, he told journalists) and their children. His last American movie, *Mad Wednesday,* (starring Harold Lloyd and a lion), had bombed here, so they must have loved him in Paris. Mike Nichols says the French adore any American director who's a little bit on the skids.

192

But his exile, expatriation, whatever it was, was not to be lived out; he was called back to the States by a writer looking for help. This writer, who remembered Sturges as the light of his boyhood, had a play scheduled for Broadway. His producers were two men who'd already been partners in a big commercial success. One of the partners, himself a writer and actor of some distinction, had been set to direct the new play. This man had hired a cast, booked a rehearsal theatre, named a starting date, and then had a nervous breakdown. He went off to a hospital. Nobody knew when he'd get out, or what shape he'd be in when he did get out. Among other considerations, the play had a hundred-thousand-dollar capital investment. Then the playwright got his big idea. His play was a comedy; why not try to get a director who was a comedy genius? Why not send for Preston Sturges?

And Preston Sturges agreed to come.

I heard all this afterward, of course, some from the playwright, some from Sturges. He'd traveled to the States, dispatched wife and family to California, checked himself into the Algonquin and prepared for a conquest of Broadway. He'd done it before. As a very young man—I think he and the century had both been in their twenties—he'd written a play called *Strictly Dishonorable,* and found himself rich and famous before he'd found himself at all.

Almost forty years later, he was back where it had begun for him, but if he was thinking of this new production as a fresh chance, he was far too proud to tell anybody.

The first thing he did was fire most of the people the hospitalized producer-director had hired. It can be assumed that there were bad feelings all around—even in the hospital—but nobody was going to tell Preston Sturges he couldn't choose his own company, and nobody did.

193

The day before rehearsals were to begin, the management still didn't have an ingenue. They were reading girls all day. Agents were sending over every lovely they could raise. When I got to the producer's reception room in the late afternoon, it looked like a scene from *The Great Ziegfeld.* Gorgeous creatures with masses of hair and perfect teeth waiting to read a few lines.

But Sturges wanted me. I knew it before I went home. It wasn't intuition; he came to me as I was leaving and said, "Don't worry," and winked.

He'd had me read a speech with a cockney accent, and the same speech with a Southern accent, and the same speech straight, and he'd studied my face the way people who use cameras do, ducking his head and looking through a frame made by shaping his fingers around his eyes. The producer—the one who still had his health—was polite but reserved, and through my heart's pounding, and the soughing of my stomach, I could hear Preston saying quietly, "But this one's an *actress,*" and I knew the poor producer was casting his wistful vote for one of those sleek belles in the outer office. (Views on my appeal range widely, due to my essential scattiness. A director once took my chin in his hands, turned it toward Arthur Treacher and said, "Isn't she beautiful?" and Treacher guffawed, "She looks like a friggin' mouse.")

That night my agent called to tell me to report for work the next morning. She said to wear a skirt, not jeans, because there would be a photographer at the theatre. She told me how incredibly fortunate I was. "You should pay them," she said, "for giving you the chance to work with Preston Sturges."

I ran up and down the living room like a crazy dog. I jumped in the air and laughed insanely. There were two actors visiting. One of them jumped up and down, too, and said we had to go out and eat and drink and overtip waiters and buy fresh flowers and maybe do something nice for a broken-down carriage horse who'd once hauled us around Central Park. The other said he'd never heard anything so childish or pathetic as we were, and he slammed out of the apartment.

I went to rehearsal in a skirt, and there was a man from the *Herald Tribune* asking me what it felt like to be Cinderella ("Feminine Lead Falls to Actress New to Broadway" his story was titled the next day), and Richard Maney, the celebrated publicist, was on hand, and Preston, in a cap from Paris and a sweater, was telling the *Herald Tribune* reporter that the cast might not be speaking to him in ten minutes—"I'm not the pleasant person I look"—and telling the cast, "I have the greatest admiration for all of you, otherwise you wouldn't be here," and the actors were roaming the stage, checking one another out.

Except me. I stood in one spot, hugging my chest to my backbone, and I couldn't get a deep breath. I was trying to fix the place—dark, empty rows of seats out front, and the stage, with its brick back wall and cold work light, and the long table set up on it, covered with scripts and half-filled coffee containers and tin cans to hold people's cigarette butts—in my mind forever.

There are perquisites which come with a lead, even if you're an Actress New to Broadway. The costume designer asked me my favorite colors, and showed me swatches of lovely stuffs. Another actress had to dye her fair hair red because my hair was blond (I didn't care but the management did). My name appeared in the out-of-town newspaper ads.

I don't remember how many days passed before we knew it wasn't going to work, that something was wrong.

Sturges had not staged a play in a very long time, but he was a man accustomed to dominance, and his own unsureness was making him testy. He would turn his irritability on the playwright, rejecting lines and scenes—"I've been around a lot longer than you, and I know about comedy, and this isn't funny." The writer would go home and rewrite, but he couldn't please the director. Sturges picked at him until he succeeded in alienating the person who'd been his most fervent admirer.

He seemed to be living in a world that didn't exist anymore, trying to remember the way it had gone when he'd been on top, and sometimes he would make suggestions to his male star—"Try falling off the piano on your behind"—which the star would instantly reject. "I don't see what good that'll do, Pres. . . ."

"Well," Sturges would say in his fluty aristocrat's voice, "we did it with Mr. Henry Fonda in 1941, and we made half a million dollars. . . ."

Once he's involved in rehearsing a play, an actor doesn't know if the thing is good or bad, and when you're playing comedy, the laughter of insiders is no criterion; the cold eye of a disinterested audience is needed. Only by then, if you're wrong it's too late.

Rehearsals went forward, but there was a hole at the center. An entire scene wouldn't be working, yet Preston would take an hour to fuss over a single word, and some of the actors began writing him off. Retroactively. "He never was any good," I heard one man telling another. "Soandso did all the movies Sturges got credit for." Sure, and a little colored boy wrote Irving Berlin's music.

It was queer to hear, and queer to think about. If some debility of spirit or invention had overtaken Sturges, if his gift for delighting audiences had burned out, at least he'd had the gift

196

in abundance, which was more than you could say of his detractors.

One night after rehearsal, I had dinner with him. We went to "21," the man at the door didn't recognize Preston, he was offended, and we left. We wound up down in the village at a Spanish joint, and Preston studied the menu through pince-nez and ordered brandy, and they brought him what they had—it was mellow as gasoline—and he made a scene while I cringed. And later we walked, while he talked about his mother, who had been Isadora Duncan's best friend, and he showed me the house on Ninth Street where his mother had had a shop, and he asked to see where I lived.

That made me nervous. I knew he'd been a notable ladies' man, and I didn't want any trouble.

As we climbed the stairs to my apartment, I told myself that Sturges was a gentleman. If I didn't ask him to take his coat off, he wouldn't stay. I was right. He looked around, said it reminded him of a garret a student might have in Paris, and when I didn't offer coffee, or a drink, or a chair, he kissed my hand and left.

I was grateful for the *noblesse*. I wished they'd been nicer to him at "21."

The way things broke up finally, the sick producer came out of the hospital and fired everybody. It said in the papers that the actors had "relinquished their roles," but we were fired. It said that Preston would "bow out," but I think he was fired too.

We were told to go home, on a cold winter's afternoon. I was wandering up the aisle, stunned, when Preston stopped me. He looked the very model of an old-time movie director, his hair, a bit high in front, waving long and silvery toward the nape of his neck, his navy blue cashmere greatcoat belted in back, the collar turned up around his throat. "I've been asked to direct a revival of *Captain Applejack*," he said. "I'll be in touch."

He phoned me in the spring and asked me to come to the Algonquin because he wanted to introduce me to some men who were going to produce his new play. I said I was busy, and Preston's tone grew thin. "Well, baby, it's *your* career," he said.

I thought about it. There was nobody left for him to play great man with. And I owed him one.

When I got to the hotel, he was in the money men's suite and they, two strangers in business suits, were sitting up straight and watching while Preston, reasonably drunk, played a guitar and sang French songs. Between phrases, he gestured toward me. "Isn't she lovely?" The producers said yup. They wanted to do business with Preston Sturges. Preston put down the guitar and picked up a massive script. It was a play he'd written in French and translated into English. It was called "I Belong to ZoZo," and it must have weighed forty pounds. "Wait till you hear her read," he said. "And she's never seen this before."

He handed me the script and I read.

"Isn't she wonderful?" he said. The two men had suggested testing "ZoZo" during the coming summer, and Preston had said he'd do it, and countersuggested that they offer me a contract, and they'd agreed again. Me, Minnie Mouse, Yogi Berra —they'd have tried to get him whatever he asked for.

Because once he'd been a golden boy, and now he came cheap, and there was always the chance that he could do it again. Do whatever it was he'd done when he was hot.

I signed a paper saying I'd act in Preston's play come the summer, and he and I got up to leave the producers' suite. There was a tray left over from their lunch, and in among the dirty dishes a couple of hard rolls were visible. Preston picked

198

them up and put them in his pocket. "They'll do for my break-fast," he said.

I walked downstairs with him to his own room. It was the size of a broom closet. The management of the Algonquin had offered him the shelter, gratis, and he'd been working there on his autobiography.

In August, quite suddenly, he died. The book he'd been writing was to have been called "The Events Leading Up to My Death."

I cried so hard it surprised me. For him because he'd been alone and unhonored at the end of it all, for myself because of what he'd tried to do for me.

The winter before (after Cinderella had landed back in the ashes), I'd taken a part in a comedy to be tried out in Palm Beach, and Preston had sent me a letter there, a letter saying things were looking "pretty good" for him in New York—"the contract for the book has been signed"—and reminiscing about his own Florida adventures. "In 1930, I was at the Everglades Club and various places—including Colonel Bradley's gambling casino—helling around and romancing a very rich young girl I would have been much better off never to have married—her name was Hutton, I believe."

He ended the note with advice about how I should approach the new play.

"So there you are, sweet child," he wrote. "Watch your makeup, give enough voice to be heard in the back of the house, and have faith in your star."

I didn't know what his personal situation had been, whether or not his last marriage had disintegrated—he had been by himself in New York for almost a year—but after he died, on the chance that it might mean something to her, I wrote to his widow in California. I said that the last time I'd seen him, he'd been happy and working hard. I said I thought he had never lost faith in *his* star.

26

L'Envoi: "A Funny Face, a Creaky Dance"

According to Shakespeare, some people are born under a "charitable starre" (and he didn't mean Frank Sinatra) but my star has been a prankster ever, alternating bolts of good fortune with cries of bad cess. I think that's true of the stars of lots of us, yet actors seem to hang in there.

When my niece Ainslie was three years old, I came upon her in the midst of some malfeasance. I can't remember what it was. "Listen," I said, "you don't have to do that. . . ."

"Yeah," she said. "I got to."

Actors are like that. They got to, even when it hurts. (And even when more practical folk are shaking their heads and reacting like the workman who helped put up the Henry Moore sculpture in Lincoln Center. Asked by a photographer what he thought of the statue, the workman spoke soberly. "I don't see the sense into the object," he said.) Actors never quit trying to improve themselves, taking singing lessons and karate lessons and lessons on instruments they can't pronounce. (I heard a folk balladeer tell her audience, "Thith ith a thither.")

For a while, the poet Yeats (who seems to be writing all the good stuff in this book) hung on so doggedly you might have imagined *he* was an actor.

> I thought no more was needed
> Youth to prolong
> Than dumb-bell and foil
> To keep the body young,

he said. But then he cried:

> O who could have foretold
> That the heart grows old?

There you have your basic difference between your Yeats and your actor. An actor admits to no incapacity whatever. You find three-hundred-pound bald guys sidling up to a director who's looking for a romantic lead, and whispering shyly, "I work without my glasses."

The struggle can begin in the cradle.

An actor named Peter Turgeon told me of a friendly rivalry he'd had with the late Lionel Barrymore. Turgeon had met Barrymore in Hollywood, and found him guilty of the sin of pride. Not on his own account. It was his grandmother, Mrs. Drew, about whom Mr. Barrymore bragged. "My grandmother," he would say, according to Turgeon, "was carried onstage at the age of nine months, and she spent the rest of her life in the theatre."

He said this often enough so it made a big impression on Turgeon's mind.

Now, Turgeon and his wife, a dancer, were touring with a musical show—say, *Brigadoon*—in a far-off place—say, Australia—when their first baby was born. As a lark, a few weeks later, Mrs. Turgeon came skipping onstage in a crowd scene bearing the infant Turgeon in her arms.

After that, Turgeon could hardly wait to get back to Hollywood.

The moment came. Poker chips on the table, cards being

202

shuffled, glasses clinking, as Mr. Barrymore began to reminisce. "My grandmother was carried onstage at the age of nine months—"

Suddenly Turgeon's voice cut in: "My daughter was carried onstage at the age of three weeks. What was your grandmother *doing* for nine months?"

Mr. Barrymore never flinched. "Looking for work, you son of a bitch," he said calmly.

Looking for work is the name of the game, and it can kill you. It always could.

Back in 1908, the stage star Maxine Elliott wrote an article for *Theatre Magazine,* advising stagestruck girls to desist from their madness. She was, said Miss Elliott, being deluged with letters from females clamoring for a "career," though, she added sternly, "the majority of them apparently lack even the most rudimentary education, and write with a crudity of expression peculiar to the housemaid."

Even so, the star was willing to address herself "to the few of gentler breeding and better equipment."

"Oh, you stagestruck girls!" she began. "If you saw a dozen people struggling in the water, and realized that only one or two could possibly escape drowning, your instinct would be just as ours is—to warn others against jumping in. That is why we shout, 'Don't, Don't, Don't,' in the hope that it may save somebody from drowning."

Miss Elliott laid it on the line. "Why go on the stage if you have pleasant surroundings and a happy home life? You must give it all up for an extremely uncertain victory that is years and years ahead. Your life will be full of small humiliations and hardships and disappointments, the recurring uncertainty each year of what the next season will bring forth in the way of an engagement, the isolation of life on the road, the inescapable discomfort of travel, of being away from home and friends and all that makes for your happiness. You will have years of poverty and loneliness and obscurity. The papers won't print fearful and wonderful accounts of how you reduce your weight or what operation makes your nose turn up or down when you live in a hall bedroom, make your own clothes, wash your handkerchiefs and collars surreptitiously, and dry them on the glass as most of us have done. You are obscure in those early days and are not good 'copy' so you won't be thrilled with columns about your soothing and luxurious milk bath while your brilliant anatomy is still sore from acrobatic efforts to get clean in the general washroom of the sleeping cars."

Sixty-five years later, nothing has changed much, the only naïve note having been sounded by Miss Elliott's question, Why go on the stage if you have a happy home life?

No actor ever had a happy home life. If the affection of those near and dear could have warmed him, he wouldn't have gone out looking to soak up the heat of the multitudes, begging for love from faceless strangers.

Actors are all beggars, and it's the smiling that's most harrowing. It's the hanging around smiling so much that ruins your disposition. It's the exhaustion that comes of trying to remember not to drop your pocketbook and whinny during an interview, not to let your voice get shrill, not to admit you couldn't play Siamese twins.

"An actor, to spend his entire life as an actor, has to have the mind of a child," Fred Allen wrote. "An out-of-work actor, whose salary has been fifteen hundred dollars per week, cannot earn fifteen dollars in any other business . . . a writer at sixty can be a Steinbeck, a Faulkner, a Hemingway. An actor at sixty can make a funny face or do a creaky dance."

Having made his case, Allen went on to perform until he died.

An actor will do anything to get a job. (Comedian Jesse White once took up tap-dancing in order to further his career. One of his friends asked another what White's footwork was like. "Great," said the second. "He sounds like a wardrobe trunk falling downstairs.") An actor will sign up for classes in technique and fencing and mime and voice and speech and improvisation and grand opera. He will live in places without amenities. In the offices where casting is done, and every telephone operator and secretary and third assistant stage manager has the power to mortify him, he will submit to indignities which cause him to despise himself. And he will go on hoping.

In the days when television drama was being produced in New York, you saw old actors in shabby overcoats trudging up to the reception desks in production offices and asking if they might sign their names on a sheet of paper (which would later inform the casting director about what actors had stopped by today, and which he—the casting director—would file in his wastebasket). And you realized actors don't store up any credit. In other professions there are merit badges for simple survival; respect accrues to the doctor, lawyer, engineer who's learned his craft and practiced it over the years. But every time an actor finishes an operation, he's out on the streets again. Literally.

In recognition of which a kindly gentleman once bequeathed a small fortune to Equity, with the proviso that it should go straight to union members' feet; any actor who has worn out his soles looking for work can get money to buy shoes.

But an actor doesn't want your pity. Actors consider themselves an elite. They sacrifice youth, security, comfort to go down the road they've chosen. And they cling to other actors, uninterested in aliens who don't understand them.

(The gap is too wide to bridge; if a play closes and an actor's out of work, a nonprofessional always asks, "Well, why don't you go on television?")

To the unsentimental observer, the actor's trade must seem very like the call girl's. Age is the enemy, unless you've made it big. Make it big and you're the madam, you own the house, you can sit on a cushion and eat chocolate creams and sniff fine old brandy. Don't make it, and you're just another aging tart.

But that's only the way it looks from the outside. The actor is reborn with every job. Past defeats are forgotten, despair is wiped away by work. The actor gets from acting what the drunk hopes to get from booze. It's why actors need agents; they're almost embarrassed to ask for money to do what they'd do for nothing.

And the camaraderie of actors banded together is the most powerful in the world. If ever you're traveling on a train, and happen upon a company of actors playing a game, you will at first be confused. Their ages are so disparate you will dismiss the possibility that they are friends. Their sizes, colors, shapes are so various you'll be certain they aren't a family. And once you've identified them as actors, you'll still be confused. Because anybody watching a bunch of players gets the feeling of being shut out of a magic circle.

Inside that circle, for as long as the job lasts, the actor knows he is something special, just as the football lineman knows that sixty thousand people have come to shiver in the stands on a winter's afternoon partly because of what he, the lineman, does. Nobody ever turned out to watch a team's owner, and nobody ever bought a ticket to see a theatre manager. So though the actor (not the star, who's a special case) perceives that he probably isn't going to have a house like the producer's in Connecticut, or a co-op apartment, or fame or prestige or even the assurance of a future, he also understands that what he's doing is what it's all about. There's him and there's the rest of the world, what actors call civilians.

And *because* it never lasts, an actor's work may be, spiritually speaking, a more accurate reflection of the human condition than any straight job with its illusion of permanence. The actor's sense of miracle is renewed every time he gets the chance to earn his weekly bread; he seldom suffers from the delusion that you can own anything or keep anything; he's constantly made aware of the temporariness of life itself. He knows he's got what he's got for just the moment that he's got it.

Fred Allen was right, of course. Actors grow old still children, fussy when it's raining out, jubilant at the promise of the smallest treat. And some are quarrelsome, some penurious, some catty, some tender-hearted, and all are egocentric and brave. They live on dreams and a good many die in furnished rooms, prisoners of scrapbooks stuffed with yellowed papers.

But if there is something sad about creaky children, there is also something glorious. Because the child in anyone is his creative portion. And there is no fun in the world like playing, yet what full-grown man but an actor can still play? Can, between 7:40 and 10 P.M., save Elizabethan England? Can whisper truths so terrible that a king who hears them must tear out his own eyes? Can reel under sentence of death from a judge, and still get to take off his makeup and go out and eat a sandwich? Onstage, an actor experiences all possible emotions without having to pay the consequences. And since life is probably whatever you think it is, when his series of adventures is over, who's to say an actor hasn't enjoyed more triumphs than anybody?

Certainly not the actor.

Once I appeared in a "showcase" production at the Lambs Club (joke about the three major actors' clubs in New York: the Players are gentlemen trying to be actors, the Lambs are actors trying to be gentlemen, the Friars are neither, trying to be both) and every night during rehearsals, the cast took a coffee break in a wood-paneled library furnished with high-backed chairs and a massive oak table. Our play had been written by a Lamb, an ancient wino, very courtly, very stoned, and it had parts for many of the club's elderly members, and during those breaks I listened to the old men talking about the days when they'd had young wives and beautiful dancing partners, and billing, and people had known their names.

They remembered every theatre—vaudeville or legit—in every town they'd ever played, they remembered lines and bits of business and every Christmas dinner bolted down between a matinee and an evening show.

But the real Christmas had always been onstage.

Onstage, the severity of grown-up questions (should I have taken a different turn? altered this? decided that?) is obliterated, and the child in the actor is permitted—and encouraged—to live.

More easily than Prince Hamlet, an actor can be bounded in a nutshell and count himself a king of infinite space.

And we get to sleep late too.

74 75 76 77 10 9 8 7 6 5 4 3 2 1